The
ARCHAEOLOGY
of FAITH

"I loved Louis Cameli's book for the highly readable account of his ancestral Italian home with its dense layers going back from prehistory to the saga of his own immigrant grandparents who ended up in Chicago. Cameli wisely underscores a somewhat hidden truth of Catholic Christianity, namely, that it has a name and a local habitation. This is no trip down memory lane, but rather an example how, like the householder of the Gospel, one brings forth old things and new."

Lawrence S. Cunningham
John A. O'Brien Professor of Theology (Emeritus)
University of Notre Dame

"With the skill of a seasoned storyteller and the vulnerability of one who is along his own path toward God, Fr. Louis Cameli draws us in to a complex yet highly readable tale of faith. We are invited to explore, to organize, and to expand our own faith through the prism of historical, cultural, scriptural, and personal stories. The best faith stories I've heard are those shared with heart and passion and this book ranks highly among them. Enjoy *The Archaeology of Faith* and ponder the role of faith in your own story."

Lisa M. Hendey
Author of *The Grace of Yes*

"In this finely wrought and deeply personal book, Fr. Cameli explores the many layers of the faith handed down to him and his ongoing appropriation of that faith. In generously sharing his own journey of Christian faith, he richly illumines our own."

Rev. Robert Imbelli
Associate Professor Emeritus of Theology
Boston College

The
ARCHAEOLOGY
of FAITH

A Personal Exploration
of How We Come to Believe

Louis J. Cameli

AVE MARIA PRESS AVE Notre Dame, Indiana

© 2015 by Louis J. Cameli

All rights reserved. No part of this book may be used or reproduced in any manner whatsoever, except in the case of reprints in the context of reviews, without written permission from Ave Maria Press®, Inc., P.O. Box 428, Notre Dame, IN 46556, 1-800-282-1865.

Founded in 1865, Ave Maria Press is a ministry of the United States Province of Holy Cross.

www.avemariapress.com

Paperback: ISBN-13 978-1-59471-589-1

E-book: ISBN-13 978-1-59471-590-7

Cover image © 123RF

Cover and text design by David Scholtes.

Printed and bound in the United States of America.

Library of Congress Cataloging-in-Publication Data

Cameli, Louis J. (Louis John)
 The archaeology of faith : a personal exploration of how we come to believe / Louis J. Cameli.
  pages cm
 Includes bibliographical references.
 ISBN 978-1-59471-589-1 -- ISBN 1-59471-589-0
 1. Faith development. 2. Faith. 3. Catholic Church--Doctrines. I. Title.
 BT771.3.C35 2015
 248.2--dc23

2014041422

Surrounded by so great a cloud of witnesses,
let us run with perseverance the race,
looking to Jesus, the pioneer and perfecter of our faith.

—*Hebrews 12:1–2*

Dedicated to all those who have been my cloud of witnesses.

Contents

Preface

THE VERDI PARADOX

*O*n the occasion of Giuseppe Verdi's two-hundredth birthday, Riccardo Muti led the Chicago Symphony Orchestra and
chorus in an extraordinary and memorable performance of
Verdi's *Requiem*. I was privileged to be there, and I found myself transported by the transcendent power of the music. What
moved me most in that performance was the intense quality
of prayer conveyed by the music. I am thinking in particular
of certain petitions in the *"Dies Irae"* ("The Day of Wrath"),
a somber piece that can be terrifying in its message. In Verdi's
hands, these verses become a heartfelt and confident plea for
God's mercy. The music of the *Requiem* speaks clearly to me of
a composer who confronts the deepest challenges of faith. But
here is the paradox: by his own very public admission, Verdi
was an atheist.

Verdi was baptized the day after his birth and raised a
Catholic. As he matured, however, he was caught up, as much
of nineteenth-century Italy was, in the anticlericalism and an-
ti-Church climate of the *Risorgimento*, a movement that sought
to unify Italy and that viewed the Church and religion as ob-
stacles to forging a national identity. Perhaps more decisive
for his personal spiritual journey was the death of his two

infant children, the only children he would ever have, and then shortly afterward the death of his wife, Margherita Barezzi, at the age of twenty-six. These were losses from which he never fully recovered and that inevitably shook whatever religious faith he had.

Still, something of faith seems to have remained in Verdi. The religious power of his music makes that evident. And that power is undeniable, as I experienced it. Pope Benedict XVI spoke of Verdi's *ateismo inquieto*, his restless atheism that kept in some measure the religious quest alive in him. I call it the "Verdi paradox," and it is the mysterious conjunction of a nonbelieving believer. This paradox is more than a particular curiosity that belongs to Verdi's experience alone. It can help us deconstruct simplistic and seriously inadequate understandings of faith that are deeply entrenched in our own cultural and historical moment.

The Verdi paradox alerts us to the complex nature of faith. The paradox warns us not to assume that we all mean the same thing when we use the word "faith." We live in a strange cultural and historical moment when both self-professed believers and nonbelievers alike often reduce and distort religious faith to conform to their preconceptions of what they think faith ought to be. Curiously, both believers and nonbelievers often get it wrong in roughly the same way. For example, they may speak about faith but really mean *fideism*, a blind assent to religious truths that makes no room for reasonableness, human struggle, freedom, or even a general sense of human flourishing. This shared sense of faith as fideism leaves no room in this universe for God and humanity to be together, much less to be in close relationship. This mistaken sense of faith can belong as much to militant secular atheists as to religiously conservative fundamentalists.

In our time and culture, as I perceive it, the faith that nonbelievers deny and that fundamentalists affirm is a flat reality. It is one-dimensional. Genuine faith, in stark contrast, is complex, richly textured, and always deeply human, even as it moves beyond itself and connects with divine transcendence.

I am convinced—or, more accurately, passionately convinced—that we must modify our basic understanding and appreciation of faith. This shift means recovering a genuine sense of faith. Without that recovery, we will lose an essential piece of ourselves. With an authentic sense of faith, however, we can find and sustain our true selves and reclaim our humanity, which only finds fulfillment beyond itself in relationship to God.

In this book, I have tried to stand before faith in all its complexity and richness. I have tried to look at the experience of faith in different ways. I have not mastered faith. No one ever does. My best hope is that I have moved a little closer to a more genuine understanding and appreciation of real faith in its richness and complexity. And if I have accomplished that bit of forward movement, it is enough.

Acknowledgments

The Archaeology of Faith tries to retrieve the generations of believers who have gone before me. Although I cannot identify many names, I must acknowledge those whose journeys have shaped my own in a more immediate way: my grandparents, Luigi Cameli, Natalina Capriotti, Giovanni Massi, and Vittoria Ascani, and my parents, John and Lena. Two of my Italian cousins, Stefano and Bernardino Novelli, introduced me to aspects of our family history that had been unknown to me. My siblings and extended family inhabit my still-unfolding history of faith: John, Mark, Sharon, Paul, Mary, Susan, Nicole, Alexandra, Blake, Mariana, and Fran. Friends have supported me in this project: Michael Zaniolo, Bob Rizzo, Clete Kiley, Bosch Praisaengpetch, Richard and Elsie Asakura, and Ruth Melson. My deep gratitude goes to Jack O'Callahan, S.J., who has so generously and so wisely accompanied me on my journey of faith. I am very grateful to those who read and commented on versions of the manuscript: John Canary, Mary Manley, Regina Thibeau, and Marcie Bosnak. Finally, I am very deeply indebted to my editor at Ave Maria Press, Robert Hamma, for his professional expertise and for his unflagging encouragement as the project developed. *Grazie a tutti!*

A NOTE ON THE TYPOGRAPHY

Although the entire substance of *The Archaeology of Faith* is deeply personal and linked to my own experience, this is especially true of the first part. I endeavor to give a narrative account of the generations of faith that underglid my own experience of faith today. I couple that account with personal reflection on the history that precedes me. A differentiated typography in part I reflects the two strands of history and reflection. I hope that this layout may also help your own process of retrieval and reflection, as you consider your own foundations and experiences of faith.

INTRODUCTION

*E*arly on, as a young priest, I learned to avoid the bar at wedding receptions at all costs, even to get a soda. Inevitably, there would be someone at the bar who had imbibed too much, who had been an altar boy many years before, and who had to have an intense conversation with a priest. These conversations would range widely, and I was certain that the next morning my interlocutor would remember nothing of which we had spoken.

When I wear my Roman collar, I find that people feel free to approach me and have a conversation about many things. And those conversations are generally not futile like the ones with over-served wedding guests. More often, they are substantial exchanges and have to do with faith. I understand that wearing a collar and publicly representing myself as a priest marks me in the eyes of many people as a "professional believer" and someone who may know a thing or two about faith.

Sometimes, strangers are curious about a religious practice or devotion, something that I might consider odd or off the mark, such as burying a statue of St. Joseph in order to sell your house. Their sense of faith is very practical and perhaps even somewhat manipulative in wanting to get God or the saints to do something that they want. Still, there is some form of a connection with the tradition of faith present here. And even a slender link can be the basis for some exploration and a deeper understanding of faith.

1

I have also sat next to people on planes who were traveling with a heavy heart to the funeral of a loved one. When they spoke of faith, they struggled to make sense of the deep loss they faced in their life. Why did this happen? And where is God in this? The questions press in and sometimes shake their sense of confidence and hope. And yet, I usually detect in these grieving souls a faith deeper than their sense of loss, a faith that seems to propel them even more intensely into God's arms.

Occasionally, I find myself in conversation with seekers. They stand outside the circle of faith and look in and wonder. Like all of us, they belong to a culture dominated by the rhythm of acquisition and consumption, "get" and "enjoy." Unlike many people, however, they sense its hollowness. For them, faith opens transcendent paths or ways to break free from a directionless and insubstantial life. But they are wary. They stay outside the circle of faith because they cannot abide what seems so closely associated with faith—brittle dogmatism, nagging moralism, and questionable religious institutions. And I find these conversations among the most poignant and gut-wrenching.

With great frequency, ordinary believers speak with me. They are very good people, generous and completely unassuming. In one sense, they are at home with their faith, but they often sense that something is missing. They may feel inarticulate and unable to express their faith clearly. Sometimes, in the secular environment in which they find themselves, they also feel vulnerable as believers. They are not quite sure how to defend themselves or protect themselves from an environment that either ignores their faith or seems actively hostile to it. They may feel frustrated by the distortions of their faith or its caricatures in the popular culture, but they are never quite sure what to do with these feelings.

This is just a sample of amazing conversations that I have had about faith. And if you have picked up this book about faith, you may very well land in one of these groups or a variation of one of them. I know that these conversations have rebounded in my own evolving sense of faith and my own identity as a believer. I have come to know that conversations about faith cannot consist in tossing around textbook answers or abstract conceptualizations. Faith is too dear and too close for that. Faith must be real, the stuff of flesh and bone. Only then can we talk about it genuinely and honestly.

Retrieving the Experience of Faith: An Archaeological Excavation

How do we ever arrive at that honest and real conversation about faith? Perhaps there are other ways, but I keep returning to the layers of history and experience that belong to me and even beyond me, to the men and women of faith who have gone before me. I begin with something deep inside of me, experiences of finding myself drawn to God as truth and love and hope. And there are many layers of experience, some of which go back to my earliest memories as a child. I am also aware that I am not alone in those experiences. Many others have gone before me, and their multilayered experience of faith undergirds my own.

I can never detach my sense of faith and my experience of faith from faith's complexly layered history. That is true for me as it is for you. And the way to retrieve this layered experience of faith, I realized, is to explore it layer by layer as an archaeologist would explore ancient terrain.

An image comes to my mind of one of my favorite churches in Rome, San Clemente. Today, visitors enter the church that was built in the twelfth century and find a simple but stately structure. This church, however, stands upon three other levels. At the lowest and now inaccessible level are the remains of buildings destroyed in Nero's fire in AD 64. At the next level, going up, and visible because of excavations, are the remains of an apartment house and small temple dedicated to the god Mithra. In the fourth century, the original church of San Clemente was built upon the second level. When the original church fell into disrepair and became unsafe at the beginning of the twelfth century, the current church was built on the fourth level.

To visit San Clemente and to explore it layer by layer uncovers a rich and complex history of faith and culture across two thousand years. I have been drawn to engage in a similar process of reflection on my own faith, layer by layer. Like a committed archaeologist, I have wanted to explore the foundations and the strata upon which my faith rests. This process, as I anticipated, could help me understand my faith, but it could do much more than that. My faith is not my faith alone. Faith is something that I share with you and with others. And so, to know my faith better and more deeply is to know the faith that belongs both to you and to me. That better and deeper knowledge then enables me to serve other believers with greater wisdom and generosity.

Explore, Organize, Expand

I want to share with you a threefold process of *exploring* the experience of faith, *organizing* that experience, and indicating ways of *expanding* or developing the experience. That process describes the following three parts of this book.

Exploring faith means, as I already indicated, an archaeology of faith. That is, it's a retrieval layer by layer of the history of the experience of faith. I am fortunate, for reasons that I will share later, to be able to go back some twenty-five hundred years to examine the foundations and beginnings of my faith. You may not be able to retrieve the origins of your faith in the same way, but you can do some retrieval. I hope that my personal process will encourage your own engagement in exploring the origins of your faith. So, I invite you to accompany me in a process of retrieval and reflection that looks to the past and the present and then even projects into the future.

The second part of the process involves organizing the experience and testing it. The history of the experience of faith can range widely as it moves in different directions. It is important to organize this history for greater understanding. It is also important to test and match personal experience with the larger traditions of faith the Church holds and teaches. Personal experience can be idiosyncratic, and it therefore needs the larger collective wisdom of the community of faith to discern its authenticity. The systematized Church teaching on faith can help to organize and authenticate our personal history of the experience of faith. Church teaching on faith also provides us with a common language of faith, so that we can share and mutually support one another's experience of faith. For these reasons, a synthesis of Church teaching on faith forms the second part of the process.

Finally, the third part of the process is about expanding the experience of faith. The history of the experience of faith demonstrates that faith is a dynamic and growing reality. It may be layered in history, but it grows and unfolds in that history. Even our exploration of Church teaching about faith to organize the experience and to enable it to be shared with a common language suggests a living and developing reality. Biblical images for faith—for example, as a planted seed that grows—also tell us that we are in the realm of a dynamic and growing reality. How does that expansion of faith take place? If faith is, as we shall see, a response to God's revelation especially present in the biblical Word of God, then that Word will nourish the expansion and growth of the experience of faith. And it will be essential to keep returning to the Word to foster growth. The third part of our process, then, will select certain narratives from John's gospel that have the power to open up the experience of faith and expand it in different directions.

Explore, organize, and expand—these are the three movements or moments of our reflection on the experience of faith. In the end, faith is, of course, a free gift, a grace. That gift, however, must be accepted and received. The better known and understood the gift is, the more possible is our full and generous acceptance.

THE ARCHAEOLOGY OF FAITH
A Personal Exploration

*W*e are layered beings. Our lives are built on strata. Our bodies, for example, and in some measure our personalities, build upon the genetic codes that come to us from generation to generation. We are shaped by a slow-moving but steady, purposeful, and providential evolution. But we are not only layered in our physical existence. Where we stand in today's world socially, politically, economically, and educationally also depends on complex layers of history and culture that reside below the surface of our lives. The layers of history also belong to our spiritual lives. Our reach for transcendence and embrace of faith right now have their own spiritual layers in a history that supports, sustains, and expresses the spirituality that belongs to us in this moment.

To know ourselves, we must explore the layers of our lives. We need to pursue a personal archaeology, a study of the self as a layered reality, recognizing that every past layer of our lives—even our "pre-lives" in our ancestral heritage—has contributed to who we are today. And that includes who we are as believers, as people of faith. We can understand ourselves as believers and understand the faith we hold by studying the archaeology of our faith, exploring its development and unfolding it layer by layer. And that archaeology can take different forms.

There is the marcrostudy of the layers of faith that is the work of specialists in history, theology, anthropology, and comparative religions. Yet, another archaeology of faith takes a more personal turn. It excavates the elements of spiritual experience that build one upon another until the latest stratum appears in focus—my faith today.

As I share my process of retrieving the layers of my personal faith, I invite you to consider the retrieval of your own history. Perhaps, at the end, you will share with me a deeper sense of faith's meaning. Perhaps you will be amazed with me as I marvel at how I came to this point of life and faith. Even after considerable reflection, it remains a mystery to me. And this may be another way of saying that I accept faith as a gift given to me, as God's grace and not the result of my own efforts. In your own way, you may also share another sense I have after these reflections: a sense of how imperfect my faith is after all these years. I believe, and I believe firmly, but I also question and sometimes seem to lack constancy and consistency. Perhaps this means that as a believer I am unfinished and that I belong to a still-unfolding history. In the end, we all share an extraordinary pattern of personal history intertwined with the history of faith. Exploring that history leads us to both better self-understanding and deeper understanding of the faith that holds our lives and journeys.

Chapter 1

CUPRAE FANUM: AT THE TEMPLE OF THE GODDESS CUPRA

The Human Foundations of Faith

$\mathcal{M}$y story begins long before I existed. In fact, it begins during the Iron Age in central Italy in the sixth century BC—and probably even earlier. This, however, provides the first recovered remains of inscriptions and artifacts related to my ancestry in Italy. Where are these artifacts found?

Today the town is called Grottammare and is located in central Italy on the Adriatic coast. The town belongs to the larger region known as Le Marche, and within that region to the province of Ascoli-Piceno. It is my ancestral home. All four of my grandparents came from this place or very close nearby.

On one of my visits, cousins took me to the church of San Martino in Grottammare. The church is perched on a hillside. If you look down, you see the expanse of the Adriatic Sea. If you look up, you see the Sibylline range of the Apennine mountains often covered with some snow on the peaks. It is a spectacular panorama, the stuff of great postcards. At my first glance, the church of San Martino appeared to have the grace and beauty of many other small-sized, older churches in Italy, and so it seemed unremarkable. Then, I did a double take. Jutting out over the door of the church was a large, white marble foot—just a foot jutting out and very obviously! I asked my cousins about it. They explained the origin of the mysterious white marble foot and, in the process, helped me begin to excavate the intricate history of faith and religion that belonged to my ancestors and, now, to me.

For several thousand years, this part of Italy was inhabited by the Picene people, one of the Italic tribes, others of which included the Etruscans, the Umbrians, the Sabines, and, of course, the ultimately ascendant Romans. Today the province is called Ascoli-Piceno. For the Picene people or, as the Romans called them, the Picentes, the spot now occupied by the church of San Martino was sacred ground. Here there was a temple dedicated to Cupra, a Picene goddess of fertility and a great figure of the nurturing mother. For agricultural people, as the Picentes were, the cult of Cupra promised some mastery over the uncertain forces of nature and, ultimately, the prospect of a sufficient harvest to guarantee survival.

What about the white marble foot jutting out over the door of San Martino? That, it seems, was the foot of a statue of Cupra, the lone remains of the temple built on this spot even before the Romans took it over. In fact, the ancient Roman name for today's town of Grottammare was *Cuprae Fanum*, that is, "Cupra's Temple."

Traces of the cult of Cupra remain even today, although, of course, many of these elements were baptized and legitimated for Christian use. For example, in the interior of the church of San Martino is a fresco of the "Madonna of Milk," the nursing mother Mary, which seems to be a transposition of an aspect of Cupra's cult as the nurturing mother, a devotion that was especially popular in the countryside. Another trace can be found in Grottammare's annual celebration at the beginning of July, ostensibly a commemoration of the visit of Pope Alexander III in AD 1177 , but which evokes the solstice celebrations of the *dea mater*, the mother goddess, which were observed well before the Christian era.

I can imagine the origins of the cult of Cupra in the overwhelming sense of vulnerability that my ancestors must have felt. They depended on the land, on the weather, and on the strength of their bodies to grow enough food to survive. They faced uncertainty, and they clearly knew their own powerlessness. And yet precisely here, in their vulnerability, they also had an intuition of a strong, reliable, and benevolent presence. They sought reliable protection, and they turned to venerate Cupra.

The pagan roots of my Christian faith are really the human foundations of faith. There is something in the human spirit that rebels against being subject to arbitrary forces. That human spirit intuits even obscurely a transcendent and even protective presence at work in our lives.

My faith begins with basic human experiences, especially the experience of vulnerability. And as often as a deceptive sense of self sufficiency or—worse—a sense of mastery or control over life tries to take hold of me, I must return to my pagan and human roots and then begin again with my vulnerability.

When St. Paul was in Athens preaching to an elite group of intellectuals and civic leaders, he knew that he could bring his listeners to the Christian faith by beginning with their pagan and human roots. He said: "As I went through the city and looked carefully at the objects of your worship, I found among them an altar with the inscription, 'To an unknown god.' What therefore you worship as unknown, this I proclaim to you. The God who made the world and everything in it, he who is Lord of heaven and earth, does not live in shrines made by human hands, nor is he served by human hands, as though he needed anything, since he himself gives to all mortals life and breath and all things" (Acts 17:23–25).

The dilemmas and aspirations of humanity are not marginal to faith. They are, in fact, foundational for faith. Both in my history and in the preaching of Paul, we find verification for an ancient principle: *gratia supponit* naturam, grace supposes or builds on nature.

To stand before Cupra's foot on the site of her ancient temple challenges me to know my humanity, my poverty, and my pagan faith. This knowledge lays an essential and enduring foundation for the Christian faith.

How does my faith intersect with basic questions, dilemmas, and aspirations of my life?

Chapter 2

The Arrival of the Romans
Handing on Faith from Generation to Generation

*T*he Romans, of course, steadily took over the Italian peninsula on their way to creating the empire. In the year 299 BC, according to the Roman historian Livy, the Romans concluded a treaty *cum Picenti populo*, with the Picene people. Over the course of thirty years, however, relations between the Picenes and the Romans soured. After what appears to have been a Picene rebellion in the year 269 BC, the Romans definitively subjugated and incorporated the population. As often happened, the Romans fostered a *modus vivendi* with the Picenes. In fact, the Romans valued Picene soldiers who had a reputation as ferocious warriors.

The Romans built the Via Salaria, the Salt Way road, which connected the city of Rome with the south Picene territory and the city of Ausculum and eventually the Adriatic Sea at Castrum Truentinum, today's Porto d'Ascoli, just a few miles south of Grottammare. On religious matters of the conquered people, the Romans followed a policy of accommodation. In fact, they would even foster local religious practice with gestures designed to build goodwill and encourage co-operation with Roman governance. This accommodation and encouragement bring us back to the church of San Martino and the site of the ancient temple of Cupra.

As I stood in front of the door of the church of San Martino with Cupra's white foot jutting out over the door, I looked over my left shoulder. There was a crumbling wall made of stones. My cousins told me that this was a contribution to the temple that Emperor Hadrian made in the year AD 125 to ingratiate himself with the local population. The Romans were happy, for their own purposes, to support any and all local religions, provided these religions did not pose any challenge to Roman sovereignty. This condition later proved to be the decisive factor that set Christianity on a collision course with the Roman empire.

By the time Hadrian had the wall built by the temple of Cupra in Grottammare in AD 125, Christians had already been living in Rome for more than sixty years. Paul had written his Letter to the Romans addressed to a Christian community traditionally situated in the environs of today's Santa Maria in Trastevere church. Eventually both Peter and Paul suffered martyrdom in Rome. The persecution by Nero had sought to stamp out this relatively small but upstart Jewish cult that challenged not only the gods of Rome but also seemed bent on subverting Rome's social-political order. Christians living in Rome and in the empire in AD 125 would be able to anticipate intermittent persecutions that attempted to stamp out their new and presumably dangerous religion for about the next two hundred years.

Of course, this Roman moment was decisively important for my Picene ancestors. Politically, socially, and even linguistically, they were subsumed into the larger Roman reality. The Romans also had a decisive role in the communication of the Christian message and faith in Jesus Christ. Even as they persecuted Christians, the Romans were unwittingly conveyors of the Christian word via the roads they constructed and the sophisticated network of connections that linked people across the empire. At some point, missionaries came to Grottammare and to my ancestors. Most likely, they came from Rome and across the peninsula on the Via Salaria. I cannot know the exact time they came, and I do not know their names. I do know that they came. And they made the journey on a road constructed by a regime hostile to the Christian faith.

This layer of my faith is complex but fully consonant with biblical witness. I think of those first journeying missionaries who came to the south Picene territory, and I recall St. Paul's words: "But how are they to call on one in whom they have not believed? And how are they to believe in one of whom they have never heard? And how are they to hear without someone to proclaim him? And how are they to proclaim him unless they are sent? As it is written, 'How beautiful are the feet of those who bring good news!'" (Rom 10:14–15).

The energy and the dynamism of those earliest missionaries walking from Rome to *Cuprae Fanum*, today's Grottammare, began earlier, even before Christianity came to Rome. It began with the Great Commission that Jesus gave his apostles: "Go therefore and make disciples of all nations" (Mt 28:19a). And Paul received his own commission as well with a particular focus on the Gentiles, those who are not Jewish. These include my ancestors on that stretch of the Adriatic coast called Picenum.

Paul speaks of "handing on" the basic Christian proclamation about Jesus dead and risen (see 1 Cor 15:3–7). In Greek, this is *paradosis*, and in Latin it is *traditio*. I stand in wonder and amazement as I consider the "handing on" or the *traditio* that has come into my life. Across two thousand years, the Word of life and the summons to faith have been handed on from one generation to the next. Across this great chain of witnesses, in the end, they have finally arrived into my life. And I, too, have responsibility to continue this handing on, so that eventually generations unborn will be able to know about Jesus Christ and then believe in him.

The history of faith moves across past centuries, but it also moves forward into the future. In this great chain of tradition, there are links of receiving and giving—all of which come into my generation and then move into the future. The great wonder for me is to know that my faith reaches back to Jesus and the earliest circle of his disciples, through time and through countless other disciples, and has found a home in my life.

What does it mean for me to know that countless people in earlier generations have handed on the faith so that I can receive it today? How do I understand my responsibility to continue this handing on?

Chapter 3

EMIDIO, BISHOP AND MARTYR AND SAINT

Witnessing Faith So That Others May Believe

*T*he earliest missionaries in the first two centuries of the Christian era who first brought the Christian faith to the south Picene territory and presumably to *Cuprae Fanum* or Grottammare must, unfortunately, remain anonymous. We have no way of knowing who they were. We do know that Christianity did not sweep over this area and its people in one triumphant wave. For at least the first five hundred years of the Christian era and perhaps a bit more, missionary outreach to the south Picene people had to be combined with a shoring up of the faith of those who had become Christian, so that they would not lapse back into paganism (more on this later).

For the end of the third century and the beginning of the fourth, I do have a name attached to the missionary effort and an important person who figures in an early layer of my faith history. He is a man whose name has been variously rendered in Latin either as Emygdius or Emigdius. His name in Italian is Emidio, an easier version to use and, besides, the name of one of my uncles. And that is how I shall refer to him.

Much of Emidio's life has been embellished with legends that are not so much falsifications as attempts to express admiration for an extraordinary person. In any case, there does seem to be a nub of accurate history or, at least, verisimilitude in many of the stories concerning Emidio.

He was born in AD 273 in Trier, present-day Germany but then one of the outermost Roman colonies of the empire. His parents were pagans who belonged to the class of nobility—in other words, people of means and high social status. After hearing the Christian message proclaimed, Emidio converted when he was about seventeen or eighteen years old in AD 290. His conversion marked a decisive turn in his life, and he dedicated himself to the study of sacred scripture. Emidio's conversion roiled his family, who no doubt had their own ambitions for their son. The family conflict provoked by his conversion to Christianity and his intense commitment to his newfound faith led him to abandon Trier and go to Milan.

The bishop of Milan, Maternus, observing the intense faith of the young Emidio coupled with his knowledge of scripture, identified him as an apt candidate for the priesthood. Maternus ordained Emidio around the year AD 296.

Another chapter in Emidio's life begins several years later. The emperor Diocletian, in an attempt to reclaim ancient Roman traditions including Roman religion, began a wave of persecutions directed to Christians and other religious minorities. In the unstable environment of persecution, Emidio went to Rome. There, the bishop of Rome, Marcellus, noted the preaching skills and enthusiasm of Emidio. He ordained

Emidio a bishop and sent him to Asculum in the Picene territory as a missionary.

Asculum was the major urban center of south Picenum.
Did Emidio also bring the Christian faith to *Cuprae Fanum* or
Grottammare? That is not clear, although it seems that he did
preach in Firmum Picenum, present-day Fermo, which is not
far from Grottammare. What can be said is that Emidio was
an important missionary presence in the area. His most significant missionary contribution, however, is linked to his death
in Asculum.

The Roman restoration or renewal envisioned by the emperor Diocletian meant the suppression of "non-Roman" elements, including, of course, Christianity. Local administrators
implemented and enforced Diocletian's edicts each in his own
way. In Asculum, the prefect or administrative head, Polymius, prohibited Emidio from preaching the Christian message.
Emidio's mission in Asculum, in fact, had gained numerous
converts to Christianity. His public activity contradicted the
directions that Diocletian had set for the empire. Polymius
asked Emidio to sacrifice to the gods and even offered him
enticements to conform to Roman religious practices. Emidio
refused to offer sacrifice, continued his preaching, and made
no effort to conceal his public presence in Asculum. At that,
Polymius, with his discretionary power as prefect, condemned
Emidio to death and had him beheaded. Emidio was martyred
sometime between AD 305 and 309.

Emidio is venerated as a saint and martyr or witness to
the faith. His story adds an important layer to my faith history.

The missionary-bishop-martyr Emidio brought the Christian faith to people from whom I am descended. As he brought the message, he died in witnessing to his faith in Jesus Christ. His death verifies the well-known saying of Tertullian (d. AD 225): *Sanguis martyrum semen christianorum*, "The blood of martyrs is the seed of Christian believers." His death and perhaps the deaths of other unknown men and women have seeded my faith. And for that witness I am deeply grateful. As a consequence of that witness, I also sense my own responsibility to give clear testimony to my faith in Jesus Christ.

Emidio's life story also opens other perspectives on faith. The struggle that faith may entail, for example, belonged not only to the end of his life but even to much earlier, when his faith led him to stand apart from his family. He also struggled with determination to bring the message of faith to new territories and new people. In the end, his struggles led him to separate from the sovereigns of this world who challenged the sovereignty of God.

For me, this layer of my faith history corrects a frequent misperception of faith. Many people think that faith makes life easier and simpler, that it has a soothing effect. In fact, almost inevitably, faith shapes choices that will set us in contrast to our world and, sometimes, even to our closest relationships. Ultimately, faith brings us and our world to a fulfillment beyond our imagination, but the way of faith has its struggles and complications.

Finally, Emidio's story contains an element of Catholic faith that will unfold more fully in later history. Recall that Marcellus, the bishop of Rome, sends Emidio to Asculum and its environs as a missionary bishop. Here we can see that faith has some embodiment in religious structures and institutional life. This is not yet the elaborate organization that comes later, but it is faith with some visible and identifiable structure. This organizational and institutional side of faith poses its own challenges, as later history amply attests, but it remains essential to address faith's social dimension and the way that believers are linked to each other. Without it, faith would become a purely personal phenomenon, and that is not true faith.

How aware am I that others have paid a costly price, sometimes with their very lives, so that I can believe today?

Chapter 4

BENEDICTINE PRESENCE AND THE CHURCH OF SAN MARTINO

Faith Lived in Community, Work, and Prayer

*T*he church of San Martino in Grottammare began between the eighth and the ninth centuries as a Benedictine abbey, an offshoot of the abbey of Farfa near today's Riete, a city midway between Rome and the Adriatric Sea on the Via Salaria and in ancient times the land of the Sabine people. The abbey of Farfa, founded not long after the death of St. Benedict around the year AD 550, became a powerful and wealthy presence across central Italy. The foundation of an abbey at San Martino by the community of Farfa followed a consistent pattern of expansion of Benedictine foundations across the center of the peninsula.

The Benedictine presence in Grottammare in the 700s was still a missionary presence. The conversion to Christianity of the Picene inhabitants took several centuries. The incursions of Celtic and Lombard people, along with the forays of Saracen pirates in the coastal areas beginning in the eighth century, diversified the population and complicated the mission of evangelization. The monastery of San Martino would have been a stabilizing presence in the zone. As a religious community, it would have served the spiritual needs of those in the area. And as a landowner with community members who were adept at farming, the abbey would have productively organized the local agricultural efforts around Grottammare.

The monastic presence in Grottammare and elsewhere in Europe was a great blessing. The monasteries provided stable environments and communities held together by the Rule of St. Benedict, a flexible and realistic pattern of organizing religious communities dedicated to working and praying. Benedict's motto was *ora et labora*, pray and work.

Benedictine communities were not self-enclosed entities. In many places, including no doubt Grottammare, monks of an abbey engaged in missionary work. The naming of the Grottammare foundation for St. Martin of Tours, who died about the year 397, substantiates the missionary direction that the abbey took at its beginning. St. Martin, a pagan soldier and convert to Christianity who later became a monk and bishop, was a favorite patron among the Benedictines. Martin symbolized the triumph of Christianity over paganism. His personal story represented the victory of the Christian mission.

The abbey of San Martino played an important spiritual and jurisdictional role in the area well into the second millennium. At some point, its land was divided, and its monastic community departed. Today, when I stand before the church building of San Martino, I can see parts of it that date from the eleventh century. This is all that remains of what once was a very large monastery complex. Now, as a parish church, it depends on another much more recently founded parish church, Madonna della Speranza, Our Lady of Hope.

The physical presence of the Benedictine monks has long vanished from Grottammare and today's church of San Martino. Their legacy and their imprint, however, remain firmly in my faith history. Their founder, St. Benedict, had a vision of faith for his community and those whom they would serve. Because this vision was so deeply rooted in the Word of God, it has endured, and even today, many centuries later, I feel its mark in my life of faith. Benedict's shaping vision of Christian faith has, in my experience, four especially notable perspectives: the centrality of Christ, the experience of community, the fundamental life rhythm of prayer and work, and the imperative of compassionate hospitality.

Faith for Benedict, and now for me, does not amount to a generic belief in a generic god, a cosmic absolute or higher power of some sort. Faith is faith in Jesus Christ, who reveals the Father in the power of the Holy Spirit. Benedict expressed this Christ-centeredness in his well-known words taken from chapter four of his Rule for his monasteries: "Prefer nothing to the love of Christ."

Benedict insisted on the essential foundation of faith in a community of believers. His Rule makes sense with the assumption that faith can only come alive in some form of community. In other words, faith is inextricably linked to our experience of Church. We go to God together, or we do not go to God. Faith may be deeply personal, but it is never a private enterprise.

A life of faith, in Benedict's vision, keeps to a double rhythm of prayer and work, as echoed in the great Benedictine motto *ora et labora*, pray and work. Faith can only stay alive if we pray, that is, regularly and rhythmically allow ourselves to be drawn into an explicit consciousness of the presence of God, who (perhaps for most of the time, accounting for the distractions of daily life) thereby remains implicitly present to us. Work, too, connects us with faith when it becomes our collaboration with the creative power of God for the transformation of the world. In this daily rhythm of praying and working, faith takes hold of our time and space.

Faith, as St. Benedict understood it, finds practical expression in acts of love. More specifically, Benedict envisioned faith expressed in compassionate hospitality. In chapter fifty-three of his Rule he says: "Let all guests who arrive be received like Christ, for he is going to say, 'I came as a guest, and you received me.' And to all let due honor be shown. . . . In the reception of the poor and of pilgrims the greatest care and solicitude should be shown, because it is especially in them that Christ is received." I have no doubt that my ancestors, who worked the land and were poor, were received and supported by the Benedictine community of San Martino. Faith, then, has meant for me that one ought to expect that believers will receive others into their lives with the deepest respect and compassion—not just as a gesture of human kindness but as an act of faith. My growth in faith is also a growth in compassionate hospitality.

I stand amazed and grateful before this rich and yet simple legacy of faith from the Benedictine tradition. This layer of my history that yields the centrality of Christ and his community and the holy rhythm of prayer and work and compassionate hospitality is truly a blessing.

How have I experienced faith, not just as my faith but as a faith sustained and shared in community?

Chapter 5

SARACEN PIRATES

Faith as Entrusting Ourselves to God

*F*rom approximately the ninth century through the sixteenth, the Adriatic coastal areas were subject to the intermittent intrusions of pirates. Their interests lay in sacking towns for profit, capturing inhabitants for slavery, and creating mayhem especially by the sexual violation of women.

The locals gave the pirates the imprecise name of "Saracens," which could include Arabs, North Africans, Turks, or Lebanese. Common denominators included their different religion, which was Islam, their general strangeness of appearance and custom, and the serious menace that they represented. The architecture of the coastal towns built in this time underscores the level of threat that people perceived in the Saracens. Towns were built not by the sea but higher up, on hills with watchtowers from which alarms could be sounded. In case of attack, protective walls shielded town folk and offered refuge to people fleeing the countryside.

The specifics of this difficult and challenging situation are few. Obviously, in a largely illiterate culture, no one left memoirs or historical records of the pirates' incursions. By way of exception, there is a record of one attack in AD 839 with the sacking of Appignano, a town at the headwaters of the Tronto River not very far from Grottammare. As sketchy as it is, the pirate history takes a decisively personal turn for me.

Monsignor Umberto Cameli worked in Rome at the Congregation for Catholic Education in the 1950s and early 1960s. We shared the same surname, and presumably there was some, even if distant, relationship between us. Unfortunately I was never able to meet him. Other relatives told me about him. Monsignor Cameli studied the origins of the Camelis. His results surprised me greatly.

According to his studies, Monsignor Cameli concluded that the Cameli family had its origin in Lebanese pirates who sacked and pillaged towns on the Adriatic and Tyrrhenian Seas. The name itself suggests Middle Eastern origins, whether in reference to camels or to the common Middle Eastern name "Kemal." At some point—the date is unknown to me—the pirates tired of sacking the towns and decided to settle down. The family split in two. One branch went to the Tyrrhenian Sea, eventually settled in the area of Genoa, and built ships. The other branch stayed on the central Adriatic Sea and became farmers. Even today, the surname is very much associated with those two locations. The ship builders became rich, and the farmers remained poor. My part of the family chose the farming route.

Religiously, these "Saracens" converted to Christianity, as a part of their settling on the land and integrating into the local culture. They contributed to a continuing diversification of the people of that area. What began with the Picene people had shifted with the arrival of the Romans. Then, after the decline of Rome, new people arrived including Celts and Lombards.

After them, as is evident in my family history, at least some Middle Easterners made their way to the Picenum territory. At a point in the Middle Ages, Germans arrived as well. Not far from Grottammare is the town of Monteprandone, said to be founded by a German knight named Brandt whose name was rendered in Italian as "Prandone."

In the Middle Ages, although Grottammare represents a tiny corner of the world, it captures, sometimes in a bewildering way, the larger patterns of history in Europe with its Middle Eastern pirates and growing diversity. These very same historical patterns provide an important framework for the story of faith.

The incursions of the Saracens, the Celts, the Lombards, and Germanic knights add a multicultural and even an interfaith layer to my larger history of faith. The mix of people forms an intersection of difference, violence, vulnerability, and protectiveness. Faith, in the end, emerges as a summons to surrender and trust.

The threat of Saracen attacks on the coastal towns, including Grottammare, was very real and translated into town architecture and planning designed to protect a vulnerable population. The climate of threat heightened the sense of vulnerability that, in turn, led to assuming a posture of wariness and to taking necessary protective measures.

Hundreds of years later, my grandparents immigrated to the United States, but they carried with them a kind of protective insularity, the heritage of an earlier and troubled history. The human struggle across these centuries is an effort to get a foothold of security in an uncertain world. In a parallel movement embedded in that human history, the struggle of faith means arriving at a sense of confident surrender into the providential hands of God. The great complication and challenge of these intertwined struggles of history and of faith is to walk both cautiously and confidently, because our human vulnerability is very real, but even more real is the presence of the living God who walks with us.

When we hear the phrase "challenges to faith," we often assume that these challenges have to do with questions of credibility. In other words, the challenges deal with the reasonableness of faith. In this layer of my history of faith, an even more fundamental challenge emerges. It centers on personally entrusting myself to the living God in loving surrender, all the while being intensely conscious of my fragile and vulnerable human condition in the volatility of a diversely mixed and often violent world.

How has a sense of my own limits and vulnerability shaped my faith?

Chapter 6

WORKING THE LAND

Faith and Cooperation with God

*I*n the spring of 1967, when I was studying in Rome, I had my first opportunity to visit Grottammare and my relatives. My four grandparents had left some forty-five or fifty years earlier. When I arrived at the first farm, a small group of male relatives, including the patriarch of the clan, my uncle Pietro, greeted me very warmly in the yard outside the house. They were coming from the fields where they had chopped wood and cleared brush after the winter. I heard them before I saw them. They were singing and shouting to each other, all, of course, in the dialect that brought me back to my grandmother's kitchen. I soon discovered the celebratory mood was fueled by a large jug of wine they had brought with them to mark the conclusion of their labors. Then we went into the house.

The ground floor of the house was a barn or stable where animals were kept. To get to the living quarters, we had to climb a flight of steps. We entered into the main room of the house, what we would call the living room. It had everything—a large fireplace for cooking and heating the house, a kitchen area to prepare food, and a table and chairs for eating and visiting. The plumbing was one faucet in the kitchen. Running water had been recently introduced. Electricity consisted of one light bulb hanging over the table.

I have never forgotten that first visit (or subsequent ones) and all its details. My aunt Parmina cooked pasta and then rabbit in the fireplace. We sat around the table eating and drinking homemade wine and catching up on fifty years of life since my grandparents had left. There was laughter, and there were tears. It was an entirely amazing experience.

The house and the land, they explained to me, did not belong to them. They and all my farming ancestors from time immemorial were sharecroppers. In Italy, this arrangement was known as *mezzadria*. The sharecroppers, or *mezzadri*, worked the land and shared the harvest with the owner. The system of splitting the return of the land with the *padrone*, or owner, kept the farmers in a steady situation of poverty. There were no extra margins that could enable advancement to ownership. By holding famers in poverty, the system of *mezzadria* also fostered an unhealthy dependence on the *padrone*, who could make life difficult, if not precarious, for the sharecroppers.

The situation of my uncle Pietro, even as a sharecropper in the mid-1960s, was not bad. The land was held in ownership by one of the local churches, and the pastor-administrator, Don Natale Buttafoco, was a relative. In fact, by the mid-1970s the family was able to come into ownership of the land. Historically, however, the relationship between the *mezzadro* and the *padrone* was generally not so benevolent. There might be arguments with the *padrone* about the right share of the harvest that was due. Sometimes, quite deliberately, the *padrone* would block possibilities for advancement, such as education, to keep a hold on his laboring force in the fields. My grandparents and other relatives who had immigrated spoke about their hardships in the system, and they did so with an obvious satisfaction that they had been sprung free from that system by coming to America.

After that first visit, I tried to stay on the farm, but I had become too American and too accustomed to indoor plumbing. So, after a while, I returned to other relatives in town. Eventually, I returned to Rome and to my studies. On occasion, even today, I return for visits. Over time, I also tried to understand these origins that form an essential part of my history and that continue to have an impact on me even when I am unaware. This agrarian history has no doubt been intertwined with my history of faith. Some important things have become clear.

Right now, as I write, I am sitting in an office surrounded by skyscrapers just off of Chicago's Michigan Avenue. This general environment could not be more urban, more sophisticated, or more affluent. Zio Pietro's farm in 1967 stands in absolutely stark contrast to the setting for my life in Chicago today. Still, my American and urban history is a"quick blip" relative to what that farm represents. My ancestors and my family were on that land, or somewhere nearby, probably for more than twenty-five hundred years. I am far more embedded in that agrarian history than in my current urban situation, even though I do not have the necessary agricultural skills, and I would never survive as a farmer. That life on the land and from the land is layered in my personal history as well as my journey of faith.

This layer of agrarian history, just as other layers, contains both a piece of human history and the journey of faith. The two movements are intertwined. Take, for example, the conservative mind-set that quite naturally belongs to farmers. Time and work on the farm are keyed to a steady rhythm of the seasons with planting, growing, harvesting, and letting the land lie fallow—until the cycle begins again. Even individual days each have their fixed set of routines from sunrise to sunset. Fixed cycles and predictable patterns enable farmers to live from the land. When the unexpected breaks in, disrupting a set routine—such as accidents that disable workers or bad weather that halts the growth of crops—farmers feel a deep sense of devastation, perhaps accompanied by anger or hopelessness.

In this layer of human history, faith can become conservative or deeply attached to predictable routines and outcomes. This conservatism can yield the good results that the Word of God identifies as steadiness in adhering to God and fidelity in carrying out his will. Conservatism can also lead to a negative response, when the unexpected happens or when God seems to be inviting us into new and uncharted territory. What keeps us faithful can also stymie us.

I remember my uncle Pietro telling me about the occasional unpredictability of nature. If the weather turned bad—for example, if hail came down from the sky—an entire crop could be destroyed in minutes. It is difficult to imagine the scope of such a disaster for people who are already living with very thin margins for their subsistence.

According to Zio Pietro, when some farmers saw their crops destroyed by hail, they engaged in *bestemmia* (blasphemy). They insulted and cursed God and the saints whom they held responsible for their misfortune. Shaking their fists at heaven, these farmers thought and felt and said unimaginable things. Today, people who experience misfortune or tragic loss sometimes question God's existence: "There must be no God if he allows things like this to happen." The farmers in Grottammare said something else. They affirmed God's existence but denied God's goodness. Their relationship with God landed in rancorous disappointment. Zio Pietro spoke of these things in hushed tones because, I think, he was aware of his own vulnerability.

In this layer of faith, even when it turns negative and the relationship with God flounders, something extraordinary about the nature of faith emerges. Faith engages those who believe in a kind of partnership with God. Obviously, it is not a partnership of equals. God's sustaining grace begins the relationship and draws it forward, but there is room for a true human response. A kind of divine-human intimate collaboration marks the relationship. Paradoxically, even the possibility of blasphemy assumes that God and his human partners have come close.

The experience of the land is finally an experience of work, a diligent and steady application to the task. Work means survival. In this human history, a commitment to work assumes an important, even central position, and that has remained in the trajectory of my human history. At the same time, the reality of faith as gift or grace challenges the position of work as the central organizing feature of life. There is a natural tension. Work is necessary in order to survive. In the journey of faith, however, things are otherwise. In faith, everything that ultimately matters depends not on our work but on what God has done. There is always the danger of a strong work ethic crowding out the prior claims of grace. All this is revealed in this layer of life and faith that unfolds on the land.

When has my faith been challenged by a sense of disappointment in God? Did I grow in deeper trust in response to this challenge, or did my trust in God decrease?

Chapter 7

FRANCIS OF ASSISI AND THE FRANCISCANS

Faith with Christ at the Center

At the end of the twelfth century and the beginning of the thirteenth, when my ancestors were farming land around Grottammare, not far to the west in the neighboring region of Umbria in the town of Assisi a movement of spiritual revitalization was taking shape. Francis of Assisi, the son of a wealthy merchant, renounced his riches and embraced a distinctive way of life centered in Jesus and the spirit of the Gospel. A group of women in Assisi followed a similar path under the direction of Clare. A few years after his turn to a more intense and radical way of living the Gospel, Francis along with some companions spearheaded a movement of spiritual revitalization in the Church. They began to preach and, even more significantly, to bear dramatic witness to their faith and convictions in a life of simplicity and poverty, intense prayer, and wide-ranging charity. And they embraced this life wholeheartedly.

Francis and Clare—like Benedict and Scholastica before them and Teresa of Jesus and Ignatius of Loyola after them—arose or, more accurately, were raised up by God to infuse the

Church with vitality and new fervor in a given moment in the Church's history. Generally, these holy men and women were not a prominent part of the structured and organizational side of the Church's life. Francis, for example, although ordained a deacon, never became a priest. The contribution of these men and women has less to do with the institutional ordering of the Church and far more to do with its soul and spiritual life. Indeed, they bring new life to the Church. That was what Francis did in his time, and its effects remain in our own.

Francis was born in 1181 and died in 1226. He spent most of his life in Umbria. He certainly left his mark on the Church of that time and in that territory. Beyond that moment and well beyond that geography, however, his spirit and the movement he generated continued to spread, and even today they have significant impact throughout the world. I thought of this when my father died last year. My father was baptized and catechized in a parish staffed by Franciscan priests. He made an annual retreat at a retreat house staffed by Franciscans. His regular confessor was a Franciscan. He died in a hospital owned and directed by Franciscan sisters. And, at the end, a Franciscan sister was the hospice chaplain who cared for him.

The Franciscan moment of my larger ancestral faith history is a deep and expansive layer that shapes so much of what faith has meant for me. So, it is important to return to the *poverello*, the little poor one, as Francis was called, to glean essential elements of his spirit and the spirit he bequeathed to the Church.

I can begin to understand St. Francis by contrasting him with another great saint of the Catholic tradition, St. Augustine. The great turning point in the life of St. Augustine occurred when he heard a voice say, *Tolle, lege,* "Pick up and read." His eyes fell on a passage of scripture that spoke to his heart. Augustine's journey of faith was intertwined with his intellectual journey. "Pick up and read" therefore fits well with the personal and intellectual movement of his life. For Francis it was otherwise. His turning point occurred in the church of San Damiano outside of Assisi, as he heard a voice that seemed to emanate from a crucifix say to him, "Go and repair my house, which you see is falling down." Francis received a word spoken to him for the sake of the Church, for the run-down church of San Damiano but even more significantly for the larger Church that had grown complacent and whose fervor was muted and whose witness had become weakened.

That beginning in San Damiano captures essential elements of what I call the "Franciscan moment" in my history of faith. Francis had a personal encounter with Jesus. It was brief, but it struck at the core of his being. Jesus is not an idea or an impersonal force. He is a person, and for Francis he became the center of his life. Jesus is someone with whom Francis more and more identified, until at the very end of his life he carried on his body the stigmata, the marks of the crucified Christ. This encounter summoned Francis to Christocentrism, centering everything on Jesus Christ. And it is this centering that Francis offered the Church as the path to renewed faith.

Notice the medium of this encounter in the church of San Damiano. It is the *spoken* word of Jesus that Francis heard, however that word was spoken and however Francis heard it. As Francis moved forward to repair the Church, he did so by taking the word and then sharing it in preaching and witness of life. This is not the intellectual path of reflection on experience, as we find in Augustine and others. This is the path of primary and direct experience in itself. It relies on the spoken word and a personal encounter.

The setting for this encounter with Jesus makes a difference. It is a little run-down church building that needs repair and restoration of its beauty. The Franciscan spirit rightly places great emphasis on sacramentality, the many ways that the presence of God is mediated in material things, whether in the beauty and order of the created world, or in sacred space, or in the visual arts or music. This sense of mediation or sacramentality makes the encounter with Jesus readily available in multiple ways. We can experience Jesus as near us in these signs and symbols of beauty that point us to him, their source. The art, music, and architecture that flowered in the wake of Francis and his followers give good witness to this Franciscan sensibility. Think, for example, of the painter Giotto or the poem "The Canticle of the Sun."

Here there is a great paradox that holds a profound truth. The Franciscan sense of sacramentality invests special meaning in the material order as disclosing the things of God. Even so, Francis embraced Lady Poverty and renounced material possessions. This Franciscan paradox conveys the truth that renouncing a life centered on material goods and embracing poverty enables us to be alert to the presence of God mediated in material things.

Francis experienced the presence of Jesus in an especially intense way in those who were suffering and on the margins. There are many stories of Francis's care for lepers. Additionally, he and his brothers continuously engaged in direct, charitable care of the poor. His faith lived in his compassionate care for others.

Again the setting for Francis's encounter with Jesus in a church building adds another dimension to this experience of faith. The church building is itself a sacramental or mediating sign of the larger reality of Church, the Body of Christ. And Francis scrupulously stayed attached to the Church in all her dimensions, even as he offered her a path of renewal in spirit and in faith. Church history records many spiritual movements of renewal, and they often followed their own path apart from the Church and sometimes even in opposition to the Church. It could not be that way for Francis. From the beginning of his conversion, he sought out his bishop. As he organized his brothers, he sought approval from the Holy Father. His renewal stemmed from the Church and was always meant for the Church, and it would unfold in the Church.

To recapitulate the movement of faith renewal that Francis of Assisi initiated, we can identify some prominent elements: a personal encounter with the Lord, mediated by his word, leading to a life centered on and identified with him, always in coordination with his Church and experienced in the beauty of nature and artistic expressions. These components contributed to the movement and momentum that St. Francis and his followers offered for the revitalization of faith and the building up of the Church of God.

Francis and his companions went in mission to the land of my ancestors and brought a legacy that is part of that deep and thick layer of the history of my ancestral faith that has continued to have significant impact in my own life. How did this happen?

Francis's first missionary trip brought him to the region of Le Marche in which Grottammare is located in 1208. Later, in 1215, according to his biographer Tomasso de Celano,

Francis came on mission to Ascoli Piceno, the capital of the province to which Grottammare belongs. He preached in the main piazza of the city, Piazza Arringo. It is difficult to imagine the reaction that this ragged-looking preacher caused, but we know that he generated excitement and had great impact. We do not have detailed descriptions of the content or the style of his preaching. We do have its basic direction. Francis moved people to meet Jesus and hear him and the radical call of his Gospel to live a new life. This was not a new message and certainly not a new gospel. His preaching, however, brought the freshness, vitality, and power of the Gospel into the lives of ordinary people. They felt a call to live differently, to pray sincerely, to suffer with their crucified Lord, and to serve their brothers and sisters in need. Perhaps the best way to speak of Francis's preaching is to say that it was a new conviction that brought people to claim a deeper faith. This was his mission in Le Marche and in Ascoli Piceno, and which no doubt filtered into Grottammare and into the ears of my ancestors.

Francis of Assisi died in 1226. Very quickly the movement he inspired gained ground in my ancestral region of Le Marche, including Grottammare. By the year 1282, the region of Le Marche had eighty-five Franciscan houses and fifteen hundred friars. Grottammare itself would produce a Franciscan pope in the sixteenth century, Sixtus V. And the neighboring town of Monteprandone would produce a Franciscan saint, James of the Marches (1394–1476). Obviously, the Franciscan moment and movement is a decisively important layer of my ancestral faith history.

As I begin to reflect on this Franciscan layer of my ancestral faith and how it has shaped my journey, a simple but important fact of my family history comes into view. Until very recently, my family belonged primarily to an oral culture. Of my four grandparents, for example, one was fully literate, two semiliterate, and one entirely illiterate. Within two generations, we leaped into a hyperliterate world that included our house with bookshelves packed to capacity and all of us earning graduate degrees. The long history, however, was entirely shaped by the spoken word.

This oral culture was the context for Francis and his brothers preaching in my ancestral territory. He reproposed the Gospel, summoned people to renewed and deeper faith, and called them to Jesus Christ, their true source of life and hope. He spoke the word to people, my people, who could only receive a spoken word. He did so in a personal face-to-face encounter and in a way that encouraged his listeners toward a personal encounter with the Jesus whom he proclaimed. So, the Franciscan part of my ancestral history of faith links my initial experience of faith and every renewal of faith, not with a new discovery in a written text, but with a living word that I receive from another person who believes. This is how faith moves across generations: faith speaking to faith until it arrives in my life.

The Franciscan layer of faith continues into the present. In particular, three faith concerns of Francis have left their mark in my life and in the lives of people close to me: his Christocentrism, his sense of sacramentality, and his practice of compassionate living. In fact, all three faith concerns are interconnected. Centering on Jesus Christ defines faith not as the embrace of an idea but as the embrace of a person. Because Jesus Christ is the incarnate Word, the one who took our flesh, there are abundant signs, images, and sounds that mediate his presence with us. That is sacramentality. And because Jesus took flesh and died for us out of love, he is also the face of divine compassion in this world that we share—made evident by our compassionate living. Person, presence, and compassion—these dimensions of faith are, I am convinced, deeply anchored and operative in my history of faith.

I was startled to see the sense of Jesus at the center as my mother lay dying. At a given point, when she was coming in and out of consciousness, she said with great feeling, "I love Jesus." This was not the usual way she spoke. She was the product of public education, she shared more than ordinary skepticism about organized religion, and she wore her religiosity lightly, although she was a believer. Now she spoke of Jesus from some deep source, some deeply imprinted connection, which I attribute to that layer of ancestral faith shaped by Francis and his followers.

Similarly, in family life, even if we did not fully live up to the summons to compassionate living, it seemed only natural to consider the sick, the disabled, the poor, and others broken and burdened by life. This again, I believe, is part of that Franciscan imprint.

It may be impossible to establish direct causal links between Francis of Assisi and my faith today. The imprint of his message and his witness, however, seems real and alive. Even when it is not fully lived out, it remains an invitation to renew faith in Jesus Christ, in his presence among us, and in sharing his compassion today.

How have I—or, more fundamentally, have I—experienced Jesus as a person and found myself in a genuine relationship with him?

Chapter 8

The Church, the State, and the Challenge of Faith

Personal Faith and Institutional Religion

$\mathcal{D}$uring the first part of the first millennium, the region of Le Marche and the province of Ascoli Piceno of which Grottammare is a part all belonged under Roman jurisdiction, and then later in the same millennium under emperors who claimed rule in the name of the Holy Roman Empire of the West. During the second millennium in a complex process of alignment, parts of central Italy, including Le Marche, became part of the Papal States. In other words, here the pope was both the temporal and spiritual ruler of the inhabitants. The Papal States never represented an entirely clear-cut demarcation, because these states (that correspond to regions in today's Italy) contained within them princes and dukes and powerful families jostling for power. In general, however, the pope claimed and in some measure exercised temporal control or civil jurisdiction in the territory of my ancestors. This shifted in 1860 when Le Marche became part of the gradually unified nation of Italy. The process culminated in 1870 with Italy's full unification and its establishment as a nation-state.

An annual celebration in Grottammare recalls events nearly a thousand years ago when popes and princes vied for influence and dominion over parts of Italy. The story of the annual festival, or *Sacra di Grottammare,* goes back to the year 1177 when Pope Alexander III was traveling the Adriatic Sea to go to Venice to meet Emperor Frederick Barbarossa. By chance, Pope Alexander's party stopped at Grottammare and visited the monastery of San Martino, where the pope was warmly received and granted a plenary indulgence on the occasion of his visit. The festival commemorating the visit continues to this day, and so does the granting of the plenary indulgence.

Some three hundred and fifty years after the visit of Pope Alexander III, Felice Peretti was born on December 13, 1521, in Grottammare. At a young age, he went to study with his Franciscan uncle, Fra Salvatore, in Montalto, a town about thirty miles inland from Grottammare and a center for the Peretti family. In 1533, Felice began his novitiate with the Franciscans, and a year later at the young age of thirteen he took his vows. Later, he was ordained a priest and obtained a doctorate in theology. His knowledge and skills prepared him for important administrative and theological duties for the Franciscans. Experiences in Rome put him on a track of advancement in Church bureaucracy. Eventually, he became a cardinal and was elected pope in 1585. He took the name of Sixtus V. He was pope for five years, and he died on August 27, 1590.

Sixtus V, a son of Grottammare, accomplished many things in five years. He advanced some of the reforms of the Council of Trent, which had concluded in 1565. He designed the grid of the city of Rome much as we have it today. He established a system of ecclesiastical governance in Rome, the curia with its congregations and offices, which largely remains in place today. Other popes had more solidly founded reputations for holiness, or theological acumen, or even as warrior-leaders. Sixtus V made his contribution in a more bureaucratic mode, and it was an important one. He contributed to the organizational infrastructure of the Church at a time when the Church needed to be better organized to meet the challenges of the Reformation, the rise of nation-states, and the missionary efforts in the Americas and elsewhere. Much of that infrastructure has continued into our own day, and it has served the Church certainly not perfectly but well.

As he began his pontificate, Sixtus V achieved notoriety for his law-and-order approach, especially to civil administration. For example, W. T. Selley draws on the 1669 biography of Sixtus written by Gregorio Leti, who tells a story of Sixtus shortly after his election as pope. The story is not likely to be true, but it captures the flavor of his administration. Selley writes:

> One night the Pope disguised himself as a hermit and carrying a large bottle of wine under his cloak, walked to the Colosseum. He encountered a group of bandits and asked them to let him spend the night there. They were roasting meat on a camp fire and he offered them his flask of wine. But the wine was drugged, so one after another the bandits fell asleep. Sixtus left the Colosseum and signaled to guards waiting outside. The next day, the bandit chief was hanging from a scaffold."[1]

As improbable as the story is, it illustrates the spirit of his campaign against brigands and the rationale for the harsh laws he enacted. Eamon Duffy has said that in the first year of his pontificate "there were more heads on the Castel Sant' Angelo than melons for sale in the market."[2]

In the end, Sixtus V fostered a more organized church bureaucracy and a more law-abiding atmosphere in the Papal States. He was a "Renaissance pope," and that is to be acknowledged, even if the term makes us wince as we think of excess and corruption in that period of the Church's history. Clearly, there were Renaissance popes whose lives and administrations gave evidence of excess and corruption. There were also Renaissance popes who were reformers and spiritual leaders and entirely admirable patrons of the arts. Sixtus V does not fit neatly into either of these categories. Perhaps Selley's assessment comes closest to catching his significance: "Sixtus V was no villain, and perhaps no hero either, but in his five years as Pope he accomplished what few Popes before or since have been able to manage.[3]

Felice Peretti who was to become Sixtus V began in Grottammare, which remains integral to my heritage. As a Franciscan friar, he typifies the movement begun by Francis that had so markedly influenced this part of central Italy. Early on, however, Felice Peretti left Grottammare to pursue studies and then take up responsibilities for the Franciscans and eventually for Church offices in Rome, which culminated in his election as pope. In the meanwhile, as he made his ascendancy in Church circles, my ancestors remained on the land and continued their lives as they had been lived for centuries before. Of course, this native son who became pope also became the spiritual leader of the Church and of that original population of Grottammare that he had left. As he exercised civil jurisdiction as head of the Papal States, he was also the temporal ruler of that same population. In so many ways, he encapsulates faith meeting organized and institutional religion.

Today in Grottammare, a bronze monument to Sixtus V, Grottammare's most famous son, dominates the main piazza of the old town, the one that is higher up and was fortified. His historical significance cannot be questioned. But how is he layered in the unfolding story of my ancestral faith? And how exactly does he contribute to the narrative of faith that I have been pursuing?

Sixtus V does represent a real and significant layer of my ancestral faith history. He is a significant player in Church history. For my personal narrative of faith, however, he matters very much. Even those in my family who never heard of Sixtus V have been influenced by him and by this and similar layers of our faith history. He represents the often tense and problematic relationship of personal faith and institutional religion.

Sixtus focused on the structural and institutional reforms of the Church as a visible organization. The point of those reforms was to sustain the spiritual mission that would foster faith. At the same time, he was a man driven by his own ambitions and frequently guided by strategies that belonged more to the world than to the realm of the Holy Spirit.

Although I cannot precisely link Sixtus V to my inherited sense of the relationship of faith and institutional religion, he remains a strong and enduring symbol of that relationship. No doubt other factors have been in play over the years, but there is a distinctive way that I have understood and appreciated faith and religion.

As a priest, it seems strange for me to say that I grew up with a very measured regard for religion and it representatives. That is, however, the case. The outer mediations of faith in its organized, institutional, and ritual side always carried great weight for me and for my family. This only makes sense. The Catholic faith tradition is thoroughly sacramental, in the sense that it depends on signs and symbols to express and make present divine and spiritual realities. So, we took religion and its representatives—for example, priests—very seriously. We expected of them a good measure of wisdom, integrity, and even holiness. This was the way things were meant to be. When they were not, we were surprised and perhaps deeply disappointed, but not entirely disillusioned. From our history that shaped our social and cultural understandings, we knew the human, fallible, and even sinful sides of life that marked the Church and her representatives. This realism about the institutional life of the Church and her human agents from popes to bishops to priests did not deny or contradict that these earthen vessels, as St. Paul would call them, contained the holy treasure that is the mystery of God's grace. A history of living in the Papal States and having one of our own as a pope driven by his own ambitions led us to a vision of the Church, her representatives, and our faith in her and in them as proposed in the mid-twentieth century in the Second Vatican Council.

The Second Vatican Council described the reality of the Church as complex, because the Church contains both a human and a divine element and because the Church holds within herself both the holiness of God and sinful people who belong to her. This calls for a complex faith that is neither unrealistically idealistic nor collapsed into cynicism by its realism. The words of the Council drawn from the "Dogmatic Constitution on the Church" (*Lumen Gentium*) put these thoughts into focus:

> The one mediator, Christ, established and ever sustains here on earth his holy Church, the community of faith, hope and charity, as a visible organization through which he communicates truth and grace to all men [and women]. But, the society structured with hierarchical organs and the Mystical Body of Christ, the visible society and the

spiritual community, the earthly Church and the Church endowed with heavenly riches, are not to be thought of as two realities. On the contrary, they form one complex reality which comes together from a human and a divine element. . . . The Church . . . clasping sinners to her bosom, at once holy and always in need of purification, follows constantly the path of penance and renewal. (*Lumen Gentium*, 8)

I would exaggerate if I said that my ancestral history has resulted in faith that is completely comfortable with the human limitations and sinfulness that we regularly encounter in the institutions and persons that belong to the Church. That faith is far from perfect and far from comfortable with the distressing situations associated with Church life. Still, this history is a gift of perspective and wisdom for the life of faith.

I can clearly approach the Church and expect and experience a mediation of the presence of God and his grace. At the same time, I will not identify the mediating institutions and persons with God himself. That would be a displacement of the divine onto what is merely human—in other words, idolatry. In fact, in the sixteenth century, the century of Sixtus V, the Protestant reformers sought to address the excesses of identifying the divine with the human. They did so by eliminating mediation and fostering a direct relationship of individuals with God. In so doing, they lost much of the sense of sacramentality that has its source in the Incarnation of the Word made flesh. Unlike the reformers, who resolved the relationship of the human and divine theoretically, my ancestors, without the benefit of books and theory, embraced in faith the mediation of the presence of God in the humanity of the Church populated by sinners, but they never identified God with his instruments of mediation. Our resolution was existential. After all, day in and day out, we lived with the Church not only as a spiritual home but also as a civil jurisdiction that could tax you and police you and punish you—and all this either justly or unjustly. Human unreliability can tax and test faith, but, in the end, it cannot void a sense of God's reliability.

I can still affirm a distinctive sense of faith in myself, something shaped by my ancestral faith history. This particular sense of faith embraces the complexity of the human and the divine coming together in the Church. That coming together of the human and the divine gives us in our humanity access to the divine. That is a great grace. At the same time, that coming together, when marked by human limitation and sinfulness, poses a challenge to faith. In the end, I am grateful for this sense of faith in all its complexity, something I have come to know through a history that has preceded me.

How can my faith in God be tested but not vanquished by the human and sinful elements of institutional life?

Chapter 9

Honest Faith, the Inquisition, and the Reformation

Faith and the Doctrines of Faith

$\mathscr{A}$s St. Francis of Assisi prayed before the crucifix in the church of San Damiano at the beginning of his deliberate spiritual journey, one of the first things that he prayed for was *fede retta*, which can be translated as "honest faith," another way of saying "true faith." In our own time, we might speak of authentic or genuine faith. There is something in Francis's prayer that invites reflection. Faith can take any number of forms. It can be conventional, that is, shaped by a general public view of what it ought to be. It can be inherited, that is, something that comes to us with the family and culture into which we are born. It can be subjectively shaped, when we make it into something that fits our particular needs, feelings, or expectations. When Francis prayed for *fede retta*, he asked for something else, something beyond these forms of faith.

Francis before the crucifix cried to God asking that he would give him a real, true, and honest faith. At the beginning of his remarkable spiritual journey, Francis was aware that genuine faith was the only foundation on which his life in God could depend and grow. His preaching summoned people to this kind of faith. Earlier, we saw that such faith had its center in a living relationship with Jesus Christ. And that, indeed, is the heart of *fede retta*.

This *fede retta*, as Francis and his followers understood it, was first and foremost a personal faith. It was also—and this is very important—an objective faith. It was something that could be known and proposed as true. It had to be as objectively true and real as the Incarnation of the Word made flesh that Francis represented in the crèche at Greccio with live people and live animals. The objective truth of faith led to the person of Jesus Christ, who stood behind and within the truths that were professed. The writings of St. Paul help us understand this.

In his first Letter to the Corinthians, in chapter fifteen, Paul writes: "For I handed on to you as of first importance what I in turn had received: that Christ died for our sins in accordance with the scriptures, and that he was buried, and that he was raised on the third day in accordance with the scriptures, and that he appeared to Cephas, then to the twelve" (1 Cor 15:3–5). This is one of the earliest statements of faith that we have in the New Testament. It antedates Paul, who, as he indicates, received it himself from others. Furthermore, Paul uses an old rabbinic formula, "I handed on what I received," to express his earnest desire and commitment to transmit with complete fidelity the truths of faith that he has shared with the Corinthians. Paul's concern for the objective truths of faith that lead believers to Jesus Christ stems from his conviction that God has acted in history. Paul affirms that God in Jesus Christ has come into the world and saved it through the Cross and resurrection of Jesus. Either this is true or it is not. In other words, either there is objectivity about this faith, or it is a subjective invention. If it is real and true, as Paul proclaims it, then faith in this truth leads believers to their relationship with Jesus Christ, the personal and enduring goal of their faith.

Paul forcefully insists on fidelity to the objective truth of the Gospel, so that people can have access to the saving work of Jesus Christ and be in relationship to him. So, he speaks in the strongest terms possible to the Galatians who were tempted to follow another truth:

> I am astonished that you are so quickly deserting the one who called you in the grace of Christ and are turning to a different gospel—not that there is another gospel, but there are some who are confusing you and want to pervert the gospel of Christ. But even if we or an angel from heaven should proclaim to you a gospel contrary to what we proclaimed to you, let that one be accursed! As we have said before, so now I repeat, if anyone proclaims to you a gospel contrary to what you received, let that one be accursed! (Gal 1:6–9)

From her very beginnings, the Church and her ministers not only have proclaimed the truth of the mystery of faith but also have tried to protect believers from false representations of faith. The pastoral epistles attributed to Paul—for example, 1 Timothy and 2 Timothy—exhort Church leadership to remain faithful in their proclamation of the faith and to protect believers from errors. Councils of the Church addressed the very same concerns. Then, in the second millennium a new instrument for identifying error and protecting the faithful emerged. The general name given to it is the "Inquisition." The word itself causes many to wince because it suggests associations with torture, vicious repression, and a backward religious fanaticism. The Inquisition, in the minds of many if not most people, belongs to a dark chapter in the history of the Church.

In fact, "Inquisition" refers to a number of initiatives, some tied exclusively to the Church and others in conjunction with civil authorities. Some of these initiatives had a purely religious or spiritual dimension. Others included negative aspects, such as torture, killing, the state's use of religion to foster social cohesion, and the creation of a repressive climate that hindered thought and expression. How did it begin? The Inquisition began as a judicial process meant to identify errors concerning the truths of the faith, to warn the faithful about those errors, and to recall the proponents of error to the true faith. The axiom of St. Bernard of Clairvaux held sway at the beginning: *fides suadenda, non imponenda*, "faith by persuasion, not by imposition." Other directions took hold in different parts of the Christian world with toxic results, and so the very word "Inquisition" achieved the notoriety that it has today.

With this background, we can return to Grottammare and the story of my ancestral faith. A layer of that history involves the Inquisition—more specifically, the Roman Inquisition. Two important figures were inquisitors: San Giacomo della Marca (St. James of the Marches) from Monteprandone, a town neighboring Grottammare, and Felice Peretti of Grottammare, who became Pope Sixtus V. Both were Franciscans, both came from my ancestral territory, and both were inquisitors. Although the Dominicans are most often associated with the Inquisition, especially the Spanish Inquisition and the infamous Torquemada, the Franciscans frequently exercised the role of inquisitors. So, the inquisitorial assignments of San Giacomo and Felice Peretti followed a larger pattern.

San Giacomo della Marca was born in Monteprandone in the environs of Grottammare in 1391 and died in Naples in 1476. He studied theology under St. Bernardine of Siena. In 1426, Pope Martin V appointed him along with St. John of Capistrano to be an inquisitor of the Fraticelli, an offshoot of the Franciscan movement that deviated in significant ways from the genuine theology and spirituality of St. Francis. By 1462, San Giacomo himself came under the scrutiny of Dominicans of the Inquisition for his teaching on the Precious Blood, although nothing came of the investigation.

Felice Peretti, who was to become Pope Sixtus V, was born in 1521 in Grottammare and died in Rome in 1590. In 1556, while still a friar, he received an appointment as inquisitor in the Venetian Republic. His work did not go well, perhaps because of his character, described by one writer as "pervaded by the spirit of intransigence and combative ardor." He was removed by being promoted to the position of consultor to the Roman Inquisition.

Before, during , and after the time that these men exercised their office as inquisitors or judges, they were noted and well-received preachers. Their passion coming from the spirit of Francis, who sought *fede retta* or honest faith, was both to communicate that faith and to protect it when it was endangered. They fostered both the personal and objective dimensions of faith.

In the sixteenth century, the great danger to the integrity of the faith stemmed, of course, from the Protestant reformers, beginning with Martin Luther. Here, too, is another connection with Grottammare that factors into the history of my ancestral faith. The church of Sant' Agostino (St. Augustine) in Grottammare housed a community of Augustinian monks. Its bell tower is truncated. According to tradition, this was done as a sign of punishment because the monastery had welcomed Luther on his way to Rome before he separated from the Catholic Church. It is said that the church of Sant'Agostino is one of the last churches in which Martin Luther celebrated Mass as a Catholic priest.

This is about as close as the Reformation came to Grottammare. The errors of the reformers were no doubt denounced from the pulpit, but the reality of Protestantism was removed from the ordinary experience of my ancestors. Geography separated the Catholics of Grottammare from the distantly located Protestants of northern Europe. It would take four hundred years after the Reformation for my family to make contact with actual Protestants, in America.

Here, in the New World, Protestants were viewed by my Catholic grandparents not so much as heretics who deviated from the true faith than as some exotic species of Christians bereft of the art, ornamentation, and devotional feeling that belonged to the Catholic tradition. Of course, these Protestants were "wrong" in their religion and faith, but this fact did not constitute a reason for hostility. They were, however, to be treated with great caution, so that their foreign ways would not infect the newly arrived immigrants and the religious and cultural heritage that they brought.

This layer of ancestral faith contains the *fede retta* or honest faith that Francis prayed for; the local inquisitors who sought to keep faith honest and true; and, with some minimal impact, the Reformation that was viewed as a serious deviation from the *fede retta*. As I grapple with how this layer comes into my faith journey today, I can detect a few lines of influence that seem to be important.

The objectivity of faith is key for me. I hold to the stable truth of what I profess in faith. If, as St. Paul says, Jesus Christ died for our sins and rose for our justification (see Rom 4:25), then I must accept this as either true or not true. I admit that this objectivity seems out of fashion today, when postmodern sensibilities relegate stable truth to another, naïve era. There are high stakes in this matter of objectivity, stability, and truth. Behind this truth of faith lies the truth of my personal relationship with Jesus and my commitment to live out of that relationship. As I have come to understand myself as a believer, I do not think that my determination to identify objective truth is, as some would have it, a kind of grasping after a security blanket—not at all. It has everything to do with identifying the reliable basis for my relationship with Jesus Christ.

I can relate to him as a great human being worthy of my emulation. I can relate to him as an extraordinarily wise sage whose precepts and sayings are worth incorporating in my own life. I can relate to him as my projection of what it means to be a fully developed human being, a kind of template of authentic humanity. In fact, there are many other ways that I can relate to Jesus Christ, none of them bad but every one of them insufficient and incomplete.

I do relate to him as the one who has saved me from sin and death, the one who calls me to follow him in an unqualified and whole-hearted way, and the one who promises my complete transformation. He is, in short, my Savior, the one who saves me. The relationship is not real if it is not based on the truth of his love, the meaning of his death, the power of his resurrection, and his very own identity as Son of God. This truth, furthermore, cannot be simply truth for me or truth for you. It must be truth pure and simple, truth that stands on its own. Without that kind of objective and unchanging truth, the relationship with Jesus Christ cannot be stable.

Now, if the relationship with Jesus Christ were just a life enhancement, a positive but not absolutely necessary value, then stability would matter less. In fact, however, everything depends on this relationship— beginning with life itself and including the scope of my commitment and the direction of my life. In other words, if the relationship is to be true and if the relationship is absolutely decisive for me, then its foundations must rest on something true, objective, and stable.

Here, I think, the prayer of St. Francis for a *fede retta*, an honest and right faith, makes sense. Francis wants the person of Jesus, the real person of Jesus and not a figment of his imagination. Francis wants— and I understand this because I want it too—the one who truly frees him from sin and gives him life. We can only get to this person if we know who he really is for us. And we can only arrive at that knowledge through faith that embraces the stable and objective truth about Jesus.

So, I understand why the sons of Francis who belonged to my ancestral territory, James of the Marches and Felice Peretti, became inquisitors. They shared their founder's concern for genuine faith rooted in objective truth. Here, too, is the very germ of the Inquisition at its beginning: a positive desire to hold fast to the truth of faith and to protect it from the encroachments of error and distortion. Unfortunately, in so many instances, the Inquisition itself deviated from its positive scope and moved forward with force, imposition, repression, and collusion with state power whose interests were often far removed from promoting genuine faith. And so, the Inquisition became a sad and, at times, shameful chapter in the history of the Church.

When I bring this layer of ancestral faith history into my own life, I do detect lines of connection and influence that are mostly positive but not entirely so. For example, I am deeply committed to the objective and stable truth of faith, an objectivity and stability so solid that I can entirely entrust myself to it, knowing that beyond the "it" of faith is the person of Jesus whom that faith proclaims. Although my faith is far from perfect, I hope that in embracing it as true and stable, I could be willing to die for it if called to do so and, in the more likely course of things, to live it out fully in daily life.

The negative side of this conviction about faith's truth is my aggravation, annoyance, and even rancor when I see this truth turned around, distorted, and even so reinterpreted that it amounts to a denial. Then, I can begin to detect budding intolerance within me that short-circuits the prospects for persuasion. Remember St. Bernard of Clairvaux who spoke of *fides suadenda, non imponenda*, "faith by persuasion, not by imposition." This intolerance can also prematurely shut down the possibilities for dialogue that could lead to persuasion or even lead to my own expanded understanding.

Fortunately, my theological training saves me in some measure from a naïve or indiscriminate sense of the truth of faith. My passion for *fede retta* does not need to be muted, but it does need to be critically reviewed and conscientiously nuanced, so that it does not lead from *fede retta*, a correct and honest faith, to a *fede esaggerata*, an exaggerated or distorted faith.

When Francis prayed before the crucifix in the church of San Damiano and asked for *fede retta*, he may have asked for a personal grace of faith. What he received exceeded those personal boundaries. As faith took hold of Francis, he was compelled to share it and impelled to move out of his world to bring that faith to others. For Francis, the *fede retta* must be correlated with the *fede proclamata*, proclaimed faith. He went on mission throughout central Italy, and travelled to Ascoli Piceno, the provincial capital of Grottammare. But he went further as well, even to North Africa and the Holy Land. At one point, Francis somehow broke through the war lines of the Crusaders and met the sultan of Egypt, Malik-al-Kamil. St. Bonaventure describes the encounter this way: "The sultan asked them by whom and why and in what capacity they had been sent, and how they got there; but Francis replied that they had been sent by God, not by men, to show him and his subjects the way of salvation and the truth of the Gospel message. When the sultan saw his enthusiasm and courage he listened to him willingly and pressed him to stay with him."

The proclamation of the *fede retta* is essential for Francis, as if the Gospel message and faith contain a dynamism that cannot be held within him but must be shared with all who will listen. This dynamism of proclamation is also important for St. James of the Marches and Felice Peretti. Before they were inquisitors and judges of faith, they were noted preachers who proclaimed the faith. All this seems to be of one piece. Concern for the truth of the faith means not only monitoring it for possible deviations but, first and foremost, its proclamation to the world.

When did I come to know the reliable truth of Jesus Christ in such a way that truly made a difference and shaped my life?

Chapter 10

Teatro dell'Arancio, Orange Tree Theater: Renaissance, Scientific Revolution, Enlightenment, and Romanticism

Faith and the Commitment to Both God and Humanity

$\mathcal{I}$n the old, upper town of Grottammare, the main piazza is named Piazza Peretti after Grottammare's most famous native son, Sixtus V. The piazza is not large, but it is architecturally interesting. One of the buildings in the piazza dates to the last decade of the eighteenth century, the *Teatro dell'Arancio* or Orange Tree Theater, named after a luxuriant orange tree that grew in the center of the piazza and that was a source of local pride.

The *Teatro dell'Arancio* is one of seventy-three theaters built in the Le Marche region during this period. The rise and flourishing of theater in the region reflects the growing prosperity of the region or, at least, the growing prosperity of the landowning class. The Renaissance that had begun not so far away in Florence and unfolded across the fourteenth through the seventeenth centuries fostered humanistic values and their artistic expression. This was also true of the Enlightenment in the seventeenth and eighteenth centuries, which had its own impact on the Italian peninsula. Romanticism in the nineteenth century treasured feeling and its expression. These economic, social, and cultural factors all contributed to the development of theater in Le Marche and, more specifically, the *Teatro dell'Arancio* in Grottammare.

I have no idea if my ancestors went to the theater in Grottammare. They were unlettered and unsophisticated farmers. I would not, however, rule out the possibility. The architecture of the *Teatro dell'Arancio* suggests a place for them. The landowners, who built and supported the theater, had their own dedicated boxes for viewing the presentations. The others, among whom I would number my ancestors, had access to the *platea*, stalls in the orchestra area. There must have been some tradition of theater even for the *mezzadri* or sharecroppers, because I do remember accompanying my grandmother to Italian plays staged at Washington School in Chicago Heights by a traveling band of Italian actors.

More than anything, the *Teatro dell'Arancio* holds a strong symbolic value in Grottammare and in the story of my ancestral faith. The *Teatro* stands for important developments across a long stretch of history. The five centuries that span from the fourteenth to the nineteenth contain important and transformative movements, including the Renaissance, the Enlightenment, and Romanticism. These distinctive moments gave rise to new forms of artistic expression, to a revolution in science and understanding of the world, and to new forms of social and political organization.

In Grottammare's Piazza Peretti, the *Teatro dell'Arancio* stood opposite the church of St. John the Baptist. Symbolically, the church represented a temple to the divinity, and the theater a temple to humanity— or, at least, to a reclaiming of the value and potential of what is human. The tension and integration of the human and the divine has always been a challenge to faith, a challenge accentuated even more in the modern period and into our own day.

Although the rhythms of life and the content of their oral culture remained largely the same for my ancestors in these centuries, the world around them shifted in radically new directions. They may have had some passing acquaintance with this novelty through artwork in their churches, or a play at the *Teatro*, or in a new machine or technology for the farm. Socially and politically, they certainly felt the impact of these movements at the end of the nineteenth century with the Italian *Risorgimento*, the unification of Italy, and the departure of Le Marche from the Papal States. The full force of this new world of thought and practice, however, would only come to the fore for my ancestors when they moved physically to the New World of America. In the meanwhile, across the centuries, these movements touched my ancestors lightly and perhaps obliquely. It may have been a preacher's words, or a turn of phrase caught in the marketplace, or the architecture of a new building. In subtle ways, the humanistic and scientific developments of these centuries reached my people and had some impact, and that impact contributed to shaping a layer of faith that linked human experience with the experience of God. This layer of faith is very much alive for me, and in so many ways it remains unfinished and fraught with difficulty for my contemporaries.

There are many passages in the Bible that suggest that God is a fierce competitor for human attention and affection. There seems to be no room for what is called "Christian humanism," faith that takes both divinity and humanity seriously. The question is this: Can you be fully attached to God in faith and, at the same time, fully and truly be yourself in your humanity? Can you be a reasonable believer, that is, someone who trusts human intelligence and reasoning and freedom, and at the same time trust God in faith?

The words of Jesus to his would-be followers are harsh and seem to respond negatively to the question. "To another [Jesus] said, 'Follow me.' But he said, 'Lord, first let me go and bury my father.' But Jesus said to him, 'Let the dead bury their own dead; but as for you, go and proclaim the kingdom of God'" (Lk 9:59–60). Elsewhere, we hear these words of Jesus: "Whoever comes to me and does not hate father and mother, wife and children, brothers and sisters, yes, and even life itself, cannot be my disciple. Whoever does not carry the cross and follow me cannot be my disciple" (Lk 14:26–27).

The demands of faith and of following Jesus seem to obliterate our humanity, not enhance it, and certainly don't seem to enable it to flourish. The path apparently suggested by the Gospel and embraced by some ascetics in the Christian spiritual tradition would lead to an annihilation of humanity. The inheritors of the Renaissance, Enlightenment, and the Romantic movement, as well as their successors today, disavow the anti-humanism and unreasonableness signaled by faith. In fact, many of them then took and now take an adversarial and hostile position vis-à-vis faith and religion. It need not be this way. In fact, I can say that in the layered history of my faith, it has not been that way. Humanity and divinity, faith and reason, transcendent concern and earthly investment—all these have come together for me, even if not perfectly and even if with tensions and unresolved aspects.

How strange to say that St. Francis of Assisi is a progenitor of Renaissance humanism. The *poverello* renounced material goods. In his ascetical strivings, he fell on thornbushes. He bore the stigmata or wounds of the crucified Christ on his body. He seemed uninterested in human reason, wisdom, or comfort, but still he provided a foundation in faith for the Renaissance humanism and other forms of humanism that would follow him.

Francis's great contribution to the life and renewal of the Church is his rediscovery and reproposal of the true humanity of Jesus Christ in the mystery of the Incarnation, the Word made flesh. In Jesus Christ, humanity and divinity come together. Humanity and divinity are not in competition. They are joined in a living synthesis, Jesus Christ, in whom we find divinity in humanity and humanity in divinity.

The moment and movement of Francis, I would suggest, unleashed a new quest for beauty in art, music, architecture, and literature, as well as a respect for human reason that could scientifically explore, understand, and develop the world. Francis did not singlehandedly usher in the Renaissance, the Scientific Revolution, or other humanistic accomplishments and currents. He did, however, provide a lens of faith on the world and humanity, the lens of the Incarnation that gives energy and impetus to pursue whatever is human.

In my own intellectual and spiritual journey, I am keenly aware of the historic struggles of faith and reason and of trying to link divine concerns with human interests—whether in science, art, or the social and political order. My basic acquaintance with modern and contemporary philosophies and literature alerted me early on to the warring terrains of faith and reason. I also knew of reactive forms of Catholic spirituality that had lost their incarnational roots and treated the world and human endeavors as utterly tainted and unholy. I saw both sides of this war of belief and unbelief, but I remained unconvinced by either position. Finally, in 1965 I read an opening section of the Second Vatican Council's "Pastoral Constitution on the Church in the Modern World" (*Gaudium et Spes*) that gave words to an intuition I had always had: a Christocentric humanism bridging humanity and divinity, faith and reason. Here is that section:

> The Church believes that Christ, who died and was raised for the sake of all, can show man the way and strengthen him through the Spirit in order to be worthy of his destiny....The Church likewise believes that the key, the center, and the purpose of the whole of man's history is to be found in its Lord and Master. She also maintains that beneath all that changes there is much that is unchanging, much that has its ultimate foundation in Christ, who is the same yesterday, and today, and forever. And that is why the Council, relying on the firstborn of all creation, proposes to speak to all men in order to unfold the mystery that is man and cooperate in tackling the main problems facing the world today. (*Gaudium et Spes*, 10)

Around the same time, I was discovering the thought of Pierre Teilhard de Chardin, French Jesuit and paleontologist, who brought a scientific and Christocentric perspective to this great question of religious faith and human values. He captured the dilemma in these words: "The great objection brought against Christianity in our time, and the real source of the distrust which insulates entire blocks of humanity from the influence of the Church, has nothing to do with historical or theological difficulties. It is the suspicion that our religion makes its adherents inhuman."[1]

In the same line as that of Francis of Assisi, Teilhard de Chardin affirms the integrity of the human and divine project in Jesus Christ, when he says: "The Incarnate God did not come to diminish the magnificent responsibility and splendid ambition that is ours: of becoming our own self. Once again, *non minuit, sed sacravit* ['he did not diminish it but made it sacred or holy'].[1]

In different places, Teilhard de Chardin appears impatient, not so much with secularizing humanists who dismiss faith and religion, but with those Christians who seem not to believe fully in the mystery of the Incarnation, God become man. In their way of living, in particular, they destroy this holy synthesis of the human and the divine. They fail, for example, to embrace the practical consequences of this faith in the great commandment of love, which is directed at one and the same time to God and to other human beings. We recall this commandment in the Gospel of Mark:

> One of the scribes . . . asked him, "Which commandment is the first of all?" Jesus answered, "The first is, 'Hear, O Israel: the Lord our God, the Lord is one; you shall love the Lord your God with all your heart, and with all your soul, and with all your mind, and with all your strength." The second is this, "You shall love your neighbor as yourself." There is no other commandment greater than these. (Mk 12:28–31)

The great originality of Jesus and the great challenge for his followers in his proposal stem not from the command to love God and neighbor, something already well-known in the tradition, but in the unification and integration of this love in one commandment. There is no competition in loving God and in loving what is human and those who are human. In fact, there is a necessary unity and flow of this one love. And those Christians who have not fully embraced this integral love present a false Christianity to a world strongly committed to embracing the human. These mistaken Christians create unnecessary blocks to faith for our contemporaries.

The *Teatro dell'Arancio* is not a large and physically imposing building, but in the story of my ancestral faith it looms large in its symbolism.

The *Teatro* stands for a great Renaissance and Enlightenment surge of concern and commitment for all that is human in artistic expression, in reason and scientific understanding, and in social organization. The *Teatro* represents the challenge of an integral faith, hope, and love directed both to God and humanity. This challenge took shape several centuries ago, but it remains today and, in our highly secularized environment, has greatly intensified.

Unsurprisingly, in my personal journey of faith, I have felt the tugs of that challenge to integrate divine faith and human strivings. I have grown up in and live in a cultural environment shaped by the Renaissance, the Enlightenment, the Scientific Revolution, the Romantic movement, and, of course, all manner of modern and postmodern thinking. Honestly, however, I must say that these tugs and tensions have rested mainly on an intellectual level. In the ordinary course of life, in the places where most of us spend much of our time and energy, I have been at peace in my devotion to God and, simultaneously, in my commitment to fostering my own humanity and that of others.

Although practically I have been at ease with the human and the divine and do not experience them as competitors for my love and attention, I am also aware of a need for vigilance and purification. The mechanisms of self-deception are multiple and devious. Both authentic commitment to God and authentic commitment to human flourishing require periodic honest scrutiny to determine if we are genuinely living the values we say that we have embraced.

How has my sense of God led me to a sense of other people, and how has my sense of others led me to God?

Chapter 11

IMMIGRATION: STRUGGLE, PROMISE, AND HOPE

Faith as God's Grace and Human Responsibility

*T*he immigration of my grandparents from Italy to the United States constitutes an important layer of my personal and faith history. Their move to this country occurred some twenty-five years before my birth, but its impact continues today almost a hundred years later.

During my first visit to Grottammare in 1966, I went to visit my uncle Pietro, my grandmother's brother, on the farm. I was amazed at the beauty of the place—the colors, the mix of hills and mountains in the background, the sea visible in the distance. I asked him how my grandparents could ever leave such a beautiful place. Without hesitation he answered me, *"La bellezza non si può mangiare,"* "You can't eat beauty." What prompted the heartbreaking and arduous process of immigration was the primal need for food. It was that basic.

Immigration, certainly for my family, stemmed not from a desire for enhancing their life but from a raw sense of desperation that they encountered daily. The possibility, the

promise, and the hope of breaking out of those dire circumstances moved my grandparents forward. There was, however,
a terrible cost in pursuing the dream of a better life, in fact, a
more human life. The cost had to do with terrible uprooting
and dislocation. Pushing forward into a new life meant a loss
that I can scarcely imagine today.

When I first met him, standing in the house that his sister,
my grandmother Natalina, had left as a young woman, my zio
Pietro told me a harrowing story. He said that he still heard
echoes in the house of his mother screaming the day that my
grandmother left. Her mother knew that they would never
see each other again. And they did not. My grandmother's
departure ushered in a time of deep grieving.

The process of immigration was not simple. My mother's parents, Giovanni and Vittoria, knew each other in Italy,
married in the United States, and planned to return to Italy
after about six years. They left Italy just before the First World
War and never did return. In the United States, they had five
children, two of them, Mario and Maria, died when they were
toddlers. Their death sent my grandfather into a spiral of grief
that seems to have triggered a crisis of faith.

I inherited my grandfather's prayer book. Of the four
grandparents, he was the most literate. I have the book with
me right now on my desk. This book with its faded red binding
is well worn and shows much use. After his children died, I
have been told, he set his prayer book aside and did not pick
it up again. About fifteen years after his children passed away,
he died of cancer. He died and was buried with all the rites of
the Church. Of course, I have no way of knowing his journey
of faith, especially in those last days. My grandmother was
left with three daughters and practically no resources. More

than the difficult economic circumstances, the great series of losses—home and family in Italy, two of her children, her husband—left a permanent imprint on her. She carried a heavy weight of sorrow the rest of her life. Still, with all that sorrow, as I remember her, she never abandoned praying to God.

My father's father did not immigrate directly to the United States. He went to Germany to find work but was unsuccessful. He made a first trip to the United States and then returned to Italy. Finally, he left again and settled in his new country. He had not known my grandmother in Italy. She was "sent" to him in an arranged marriage. They had four children and some measure of financial success. Within about ten years, they were able to build their own house, a bungalow. The household was Catholic, of course. My grandfather and namesake, as best as I can determine, participated only infrequently in church services. His wife and children did participate, however, and I think that he depended on their prayers as well as those of his sisters who had also immigrated here.

Despite all the loss and upheaval that immigration provoked, it largely fulfilled the promise and hope of a better and more sustainable life. With two generations born in the United States, the educational level and financial well-being of family members increased dramatically. After nearly a hundred years, there are now three generations born in the United States. The process of reconstituting life and rooting it in this country is complete. The measure of that completion—in my estimation—is the fact of forgetfulness. At this point, everything that I have narrated is virtually out of view of living family members. My own tenuous grasp of this history is a result of being the firstborn of the second American generation and being the only one now living who has a linguistic connection with the grandparents. America, unlike the nations of Europe, seems to be a nation built on short memories. What remains of the Old World culture in our family is its food, an expressive style of communication, perhaps stronger than average family cohesion, and a more or less consistent religious identity as Catholics. We are fully and completely here as a family. This is the only home we have known.

Basic needs for food and work pushed my grandparents to come to the United States. These are empirically measurable reasons that explain why they undertook this hugely complicated and disruptive process. Another force, I believe, was also in play. This was the spiritual energy that enabled the immigration to happen and enabled the building of a new life in this country. Many people might characterize this spiritual energy not only for my family but for many immigrant people as a triple form of faith: faith in God, faith in America, and faith in themselves. Faith in a God of providence who leads us forward in life is foundational for so many of us. Faith in America as a land of opportunity is deeply embedded in the national psyche. Faith in ourselves as resourceful and self-reliant certainly is the way that we want to view ourselves, even if we are at times, in fact, far more hesitant than confident. I think that triple faith—in God, in America, in oneself—was probably operative in some measure for my grandparents. I do not know how I could ever exactly determine what that triple faith actually and practically meant for my grandparents. There is, however, another side of their faith that I can identify much more precisely.

Two sides of my grandparents' human experience became infused with faith, even if they could not explicitly articulate their experience or give expression to the faith that it generated. The reality is clear to me. They acutely experienced their dependency and vulnerability, as I have already described it. And this experience prompted them to make a decision and take action. Here, then, in their decision and action was another experience, the experience of their agency and responsibility. They may have truly been dependent and vulnerable, but they were not just pawns of historical-economic forces. They could become active players who could responsibly direct their own lives and change the future course of history for their children and future generations.

In the middle of the experience of dependency and vulnerability, my grandparents discovered an opportunity, a gift or grace beyond the limitations of their situation: the possibility of new life. At the same time, they understood that this gift could only be real for them if they acted on it, decided to embrace it in their freedom with all the consequences, both positive and negative, that would follow. This double experience of grace and freedom locates us in the realm of faith. And so, what belonged to the faith of my immigrant grandparents became a layer of my own faith, as I came to understand it.

The impact of my grandparents' immigration has occupied my attention, as I try to understand its personal and spiritual impact. The recent immigration of people to the Chicago area, especially from Mexico and Latin America as well as Asia, has triggered and intensified this reflection for me. In my very early years, my family had no conscious appraisal of what the immigration meant and what impact it exercised. In a rush to become American, they suppressed that history of transition, and they preserved a few cultural remnants of the Old World, mainly in their home. They rarely expressed their culture of origin in public.

So, language was quickly lost. Even names of grandparents and other relatives in Italy were forgotten in a generation. Perhaps, in addition to the rush to Americanize, the pain of leaving home and the struggle to reconstitute a new life also fostered forgetfulness about the painful process of immigration.

Although the immigration experience may be largely lost to conscious memory, I have come to know, even if imperfectly and incompletely, how much that experience has stamped my life and my faith. It might seem that for me and those of my cohort—the second generation born in the United States—these things would not matter that much, but they do. They matter intensely. Four aspects have emerged as especially important for me: the contrast between tradition and innovation, the polarity of anxiety and confident hope, the conjunction of graced opportunities and personal responsibility, and, finally, seeing the world itself as the stage for life and faith's unfolding.

Earlier, when I reflected on my ancestors who worked the land for centuries as farmers, I linked their work with its predictable cycles to a deeply imbedded conservative sense of life and an attachment to tradition. I have discovered that agrarian-based cultural DNA in myself. Certainly, in their own way, my grandparents understood themselves as conservators of tradition. That self-understanding, however, expanded with the daring and novel move that they made to leave home and come to a new country. As traditional as they were, they also embraced innovation. I got to know my paternal grandfather just a little before he died when I was four years old, but the memory of his devotion to the Chicago Cubs was stamped in my psyche. Within a decade of his arrival, he aligned himself with the sports of this new world. More significantly, these former sharecroppers quickly moved to home ownership—a real novelty for them.

In the realm of faith, I have experienced—and I am not alone in this—the contrast and interplay of both tradition and innovation.

Perhaps this is best illustrated through a comment that Cardinal Carlo Martini made shortly before his death. He challenged the Church to communicate what he called "the freshness of the Gospel" to the world. I knew exactly what he meant. The Gospel when thoughtfully and passionately presented has a unique capacity to cast new light on the human condition. What seemed so sure and certain is turned around. New possibilities for relationships, for hope, and for enduring love become real. The Gospel, which is deeply traditional and meant to be preserved in all its integrity, becomes the source of new wisdom and new hope in every generation. All this I have taken very personally. I will jealousy guard and preserve what is handed on in the Gospel tradition. At the same time, I am not content with some fossilized representation of the Gospel. It must carry creative and innovative force and power. So, for example, in our digital age, the Gospel should redirect us to true and new depths of human communication and communion. Similarly, in a time when we are especially conscious of the earth's fragility, the Gospel should move us to new paths of stewardship for the earth's resources.

This contrast of tradition and innovation evident in the story of my grandparents and in my own experience of faith has strong echoes in the biblical presentation of faith. For example, Abraham, a solid believer in God and seventy-five years old, heard God's call: "Go from your country and your kindred and your father's house to the land that I will show you" (Gen 12:1). Leaning entirely on his faith, he embraced this utterly new direction, and he went. In the New Testament, St. Paul held fast to the tradition he received and, at the same time, embraced a pervasive vision of novelty in Jesus Christ: "So if anyone is in Christ, there is a new creation: everything old has passed away; see, everything has become new!" (2 Cor 5:17).

The contrast of tradition and innovation assures me that faith is alive. The mix of family history and faith history confirms this. Faith is rooted, but faith is also dynamic. The contrast and conjunction of tradition and innovation stem from history and certainly contain seeds of tension. In an even more dramatic way, the polarity of anxiety and confident hope—also rooted in history—gives rise to an ongoing struggle to find a spiritual integration.

Anxiety belongs to the human condition. As I understand it, anxiety has to do with fear and a feeling of unease because of a sense of impending loss. Some people are more anxious than others, perhaps because it belongs to their physiology, the way that they are neurologically wired. Others are anxious because they have been taught to fear impending loss that will shatter their lives and not leave them the same ever again. I think that this second learned anxiety has been a prominent feature of my family. Furthermore, I believe that it is rooted in the experience of immigration. It has deep consequences for faith. Let me explain.

A bit of neurotic anxiety probably belongs to everyone. For a long time, I thought that the pervasive family feeling of impending loss belonged to that universal human experience. Only with time and a wider range of experience have I come to understand that our anxiety amounted to something more than a universal feature of life.

All anxiety is anticipatory. It glimpses disaster ahead, down the road. Our anxiety, I later realized, had an apocalyptic quality to it, a dramatically intense tone that seemed odd in contrast to the experience of other people. Rarely, if ever, would anyone in the family say, "Don't worry. Everything will be all right." The assumption was quite the opposite—looming disaster was certain. Of course, there were disasters and losses, but they were never as frequent or as dire as our feelings of anxiety had predicted. I realized that many other people did not share these feelings as we experienced them. And then I wondered: Where did this awful anxiety originate?

My analysis led me back to anxiety as an anticipation of loss. Then, one day, I recognized the key to understanding our anxiety. In so many ways, what we held as a feeling of anticipation had in fact already happened. The loss of family, of familiar terrain, of language, of customary ways, of children to death, of many other things as well—all this had already happened. From those past losses, we began to envision our future losses, and our anxiety was born as a lens through which we would view life.

Strangely, although this anxiety caused and continues to cause feelings of dread, and although it has sometimes been inappropriately medicated with alcohol or drugs, it has not generally halted my family members. We have moved forward. We have made advances. Paradoxically, with our anxiety about life, we also carry with us a sense of confident hope. And that, indeed, is a paradox that does not yield to easy explanation.

We have hope in opportunities and confidence in our ability to seize those opportunities. This does not mean that we feel less anxious because of our confident hope. It does mean that anxiety does not render us immobile.

Faith translates this experience as participation in the dying and rising of Christ, the paschal mystery. In Christ, we die. In him, we truly experience loss in the extreme. From the Cross, Jesus cried out, "My God, my God, why have you forsaken me?" (Mk 15:34). Then, with him in his resurrection, we strive to move beyond our anxieties and doubts to a point of hope and confidence centered in him. In Luke's gospel, the risen Jesus appears to his disciples and says, "Why are you frightened, and why do doubts arise in your hearts? Look at my hands and my feet; see that it is I myself" (Lk 24:38–39). Unlike the frequently depicted simplistic and reductive understandings of faith, the polarity of real anxiety and real confident hope demonstrates the complex experience of faith, an experience that truly corresponds to the intricacies of being a genuine human being in history. In my story of faith, this experience is linked to the momentous process of immigration.

The contrast between tradition and innovation and the polarity of anxiety and confident hope are the first two elements that capture the personal and spiritual impact of the immigration experience. The third element is related to these two but also differs from them. It is the conjunction of graced opportunities and personal responsibility.

The clichéd description of America as "the land of opportunity" reflects a reality. For some four hundred years, immigrants have been drawn to this land because they sensed the possibilities for a better life in this new setting. They saw the opportunities as a gift or a grace that could lift them up and create a better life for themselves and their children. Of course, they also knew that they had to take responsibility for those opportunities. They had to work and, generally, work very hard to make those opportunities become full-fledged realities.

My grandparents would never have spoken of their experience as a conjunction of gift and responsibility or of grace and work. That language did not correspond to their conceptual frameworks. On the other hand, opportunity and responsibility and grace and work were deeply embedded in their experience, so that they encountered this reality every day. Daily—on the job, in schools, in neighborhoods, in the shops, in the home that they owned—they knew that something was given to them. At the same time, they claimed what was given and responded to it with their efforts.

My grandparents—and the generations following them—had and cultivated a strong work ethic. In addition to this, however, they had a grace ethic. In other words, what drew them to work and what drew them to immigrate in the first place was a sense of opportunity that was both a gift and a promise. This conjunction of opportunity and responsibility belongs to my history but continues to have a shaping impact on my journey of faith today.

Beginning with St. Paul, every Christian including me has had to reckon with the foundational primacy of grace, God's gift in our lives. "For by grace you have been saved through faith, and this is not your own doing; it is the gift of God—not the result of works" (Eph 2:8–9). At the same time, truly believing means responding to the gift with a faith that is active and "brought to completion by . . . works" (Jas 2:22).

Across Christian history from Paul and Augustine to the present moment—and, even more particularly, across my own life—the integration of grace and works remains a challenge and a forever-unfinished task. It seems easier to work hard to stake out a certain level of achievement in this world. I did not emerge from a social class of leisure, which could just take time slowly and appreciate what life had to offer. The family history points me more in the direction of work. Still, the same family history in the experience of immigration reveals the priority of graced opportunity in this new land, which was foundational for the commitment to work and achieve. So, my personal and faith journey can advance with my strivings but even more with my reflection on the gift or grace beneath the strivings.

The fourth and final element of impact from the immigration experience on the journey of life and faith has to do with where that journey unfolds. It is the world itself and the world's history. This world stage for life and faith represents an astonishing expansion of vision in my ancestral history.

For at least three millennia, my ancestors lived and stayed within a twenty mile radius of their home. Strangers came and invaded—for example, the Romans, the Celts, and the Lombards. Pirate incursions brought a Middle East element into the local population. Until the beginning of the twentieth century, however, the people of Grottammare stayed put. The world of my ancestors was a small world. That all changed with their immigration.

Traveling thousands of miles from home meant entrance into an unimaginably larger world than my ancestors had ever experienced. Coming to the United States, they encountered not just new terrain but also new people, a diversity of cultures and races. Although my grandparents clustered with others from their hometown and its environs, their *paesani*, they also met the daily reality of diversity in America. I can distinctly remember that within a few blocks of my grandmother's house there were people from Poland, Russia, Lithuania, Greece, and Mexico, as well as African Americans. A few miles east were the Dutch farmers, and two miles west there were Germans, Irish, and Swedes. Ironically, only in America did my grandparents meet Italians from other regions of Italy, such as Lazio, Calabria, and Sicily. There was also a diversity of religious expressions, including, of course, Catholicism, Greek Orthodoxy, various Protestant denominations, and Judaism.

Obviously, this diversity expanded their view of the world. My grandparents and their peers broke through the boundaries of the small town and culturally homogeneous environment that belonged to their birth and early formation. They viewed their new world with a mix of suspicion and curiosity. As generations settled in this country, we came to assume this large and diverse world as "normal."

This expanded world sense also shaped faith, especially in its Catholic dimensions and its commitment to the world's transformation. Catholicism remains truest to itself when it extends a universal embrace to all people. In the words of St. Peter in the Acts of the Apostles: "I truly understand that God shows no partiality, but in every nation anyone who fears him and does what is right is acceptable to him" (Acts 10:34–35). The universal mission reverberates in the Great Commission at the end of Matthew's gospel: "Go therefore and make disciples of all nations" (Mt 28:19a). These senses of diversity and worldwide outreach coalesce in the Church's description of her own identity in the Second Vatican Council: "The Church, in Christ, is in the nature of sacrament—a sign and instrument, that is, of communion with God and of the unity among all people" (*Lumen Gentium*, I).

I can clearly detect on my own journey of faith the personal and spiritual impact of the diversity and world vision that took hold of my grandparents in this new world. I believe that the shock waves of that encounter with a larger and greatly diverse world after millennia of provincial living continue to reverberate and shape me. In faith, I hold and have closely held the realities of diversity and unity and the need for a worldwide perspective.

The world is not only a terrain of diversity, as the immigration experience revealed. It is also the place where we take action, where decisions are made, where what we believe can come alive and make a difference. The world as the field for action is also a perspective that I have gained from my grandparents' immigration experience.

I am certain that my grandparents did not see themselves as actors on the world's stage, but they were. Their role was small, and they were joined by countless others in the grand migratory movements of history. Still, they took their needs and their aspirations and made decisions that brought them to take action on that large stage of the world and its history. They unfolded what mattered most to them in this grand setting. In doing that, they set a pattern—as I have detected—for my own journey of faith.

I have always felt a natural fit between how I believe and how I engage the world. The human and the holy have not only been compatible but are also inextricably linked together for me. Instinctively, I knew even before I read the words of the Second Vatican Council the truth of its declaration: "Christians cherish a feeling of deep solidarity with the human race and its history" (*Gaudium et Spes*, I). I have felt out of sync with a more typically American attitude that prefers religion and faith to be private matters. Faith, which matters so much to me, must find some expression and engagement in the world. I easily understand the passion of Dorothy Day, who had to bring faith to bear on the transformation of the world.

My immigrant grandparents may have been more immediately concerned about changing their world rather than changing the world at large. Yet, they and others did change the world. As a believer, I have understood faith's transformative power in my life but also beyond my life in the world. In this, I think that I am staying faithful to the words of Jesus in his Sermon on the Mount:

> You are the light of the world. A city built on a hill cannot be hid. No one after lighting a lamp puts it under the bushel basket, but on the lampstand, and it gives light to all in the house. In the same way, let your light shine before others, so that they may see your good works and give glory to your Father in heaven. (Mt 5:14–16)

As I conclude these reflections on this extraordinary layer of personal and faith history, I am astonished at its richness. Certainly, my grandparents would never have envisioned—and even less so, articulated—the implications of their decision to leave their home and come to this country. Still, their human journey has significantly shaped the faith journey of those who follow them. I have identified four significant aspects that rebounded on my faith journey—the contrast between tradition and innovation, the polarity of anxiety and confident hope, the conjunction of graced opportunities and personal responsibility, and seeing the world itself as the stage for faith's unfolding. For now, I have identified four aspects, but in the future I think even more will become evident to me.

When has faith enabled me to take risks and move forward? When has faith summoned me to hold fast to what I believe?

Chapter 12

FAITH GIVEN AND THEN CLAIMED: EARLY YEARS

The Grace of Faith Held by the Community of Faith

At this point in my archeological explorations, things take a different turn. I am in the most recent strata, which belong to my own life. Autobiographical reflections seem less objective and subject to more distortions and omissions than a straightforward rendering of past history. Even so, looking at my own life is absolutely necessary to complete the reflection on faith.

I have a small photograph of my very young mother and my aunt Rita, who was my godmother, holding me on the day of my Baptism. My eyes are wide open, and I seem to be very much at peace resting in their arms. The picture captures the earliest moment in my faith journey and how it began. On September 3, 1944, my family and my godparents brought me to San Rocco Church for Baptism. It was not my idea to ask for Baptism, although from the photo it seems that I did not mind. And here, in my infant Baptism, begins a whole series of interesting questions and explorations of faith.

Baptism is *par excellence* the sacrament of faith. At the end of Mark's gospel, Jesus tells his followers who will carry on his mission: "The one who believes and is baptized will be saved" (Mk 16:16a). The sequence and the causal line seem clear: you believe, and because you believe you *then* seek Baptism. This leads to the question of infant Baptism, which has vexed different churches in the Christian tradition. A number of Protestant churches do not baptize infants but wait for individuals to make a profession of faith and a subsequent request for Baptism. Other Protestant churches do baptize infants, and, of course, this is true of the Catholic Church.

What is the logic of this path of Baptism and faith for infants, which was my path? It begins with the necessity of Baptism or, more particularly, the necessity of baptismal regeneration, being born again, as Jesus explains it to Nicodemus: "Very truly, I tell you, no one can enter the kingdom of God without being born of water and Spirit" (Jn 3:5). All humanity needs that regeneration, even when they are not conscious of the need, as I was not conscious of it in my infant state.

God's grace is both abundant and prior to our action. Again, Jesus speaking to Nicodemus says, "[God] gives the Spirit without measure" (Jn 3:34b). There is no rationing of God's Holy Spirit. By God's abundant and prior grace, my family's faith brought me to Baptism. St. Augustine, however, says that what matters even more than the family's faith is the faith of Mother Church in which children are baptized: "The whole Church is the mother of all and the mother of each."

Clearly, my parents, grandparents, and godparents wanted "to get me baptized," as they would have said. Their motives may not have been entirely clear, and their own faith was more or less informed and explicitly formed. I, however, rode into Baptism on the powerful matrix of the believing Church, the spouse of Jesus Christ to whom I was attached through this great sacrament. That ride into Baptism did have consequences later, and they had to do with my personal faith.

Baptism always remains the great sacrament of faith. Although in my infancy I depended on the faith of the Church and of my family, I also needed to claim that faith in Jesus Christ as my own and so, with my free assent and consent, ratify my Baptism that took place about six weeks after my birth. Arriving at that point of personal faith depended, however, on several stages.

I am fascinated, for example, by the very earliest stage of moving toward personal faith—infant catechesis. The *General Directory for Catechesis* speaks of this formation or preparation of infants that will provide the foundations for them to claim one day their personal faith. The translated text is awkward and a bit technical, but its directions for preparing and moving infants to full personal faith are astonishing. It reads: "The catechetical process in infancy is eminently educational. It seeks to develop those human resources which provide an anthropological basis for the life of faith, a sense of trust, of freedom, of self-giving, of invocation, and of joyful participation" (*GDC*, 178). From the earliest weeks of life, formation for personal faith begins in building trust, in encouraging freedom, in inviting invocation or a communication that calls out, and in fostering joyful participation that is the stuff of play. You can easily see here the heart of faith being formed for loving and free surrender to God that will find expression in prayer and celebration. I am amazed at how early these first steps toward a personal faith are. And they ring so true. In my own personal history, of course, I have practically no conscious memory of these earliest steps. In retrospect, however, I must acknowledge that these steps must have been present because of my faith that took shape later. My mother played a pivotal role in this process.

My mother had me when she was very young, just short of her eighteenth birthday. It was a different time, and young people may have matured earlier. Her life circumstances, especially the early death of her father, also pushed her process of maturation forward. Still, she was a teenager and still very much in the process of her personal development. In later years, we talked about this and what it meant to be a mother at seventeen. She certainly felt the challenges of being a very young mother, and she could only rely on limited help from my father, who had to work two full-time jobs because of our very straitened economic circumstances.

In a related way, my professional work later led me to study the relationship of infants and their mothers in the work of the British pediatrician and psychoanalyst D. W. Winnicott. He plotted out the decisive and lifelong importance of that relationship for the infant's development. His perspective was attachment and detachment and what he called "the good enough mother." When it all worked well, the results could be identified in the infant: trust, freedom, and a sense of self—elements of one piece with the foundations for personal faith. From all of this, what could I conclude about my earliest formation and preparation as an infant for personal faith?

I can conclude that my mother, despite all her limitations, which she readily acknowledged, belonged to that august category of D. W. Winnicott, "the good enough mother." Somehow, she helped me achieve not perfect but sufficient trust. With her guidance, I also felt freedom, so that I began to explore the world and form relationships, a very rudimentary form of self-giving. Certainly, she moved me to joyful participation, that is, to playing and enjoying interaction with other children and adults. In fact, the memories of that "joyful participation" may be the most vivid of my earliest years.

This stratum of my infant history, although difficult to access directly, decisively shaped the foundations for my explicit personal faith that followed. Just as the photograph shows my mother carrying me to my Baptism, so, too, she carried me in infancy into the development of self, trust, freedom, and joy that became the supportive personal structure of my faith.

Late infancy and early childhood signaled another shift in my faith journey. Explicit and tangible elements of faith and religion entered into my life. One year—I was probably three and a half or four years old—we went to the local Woolworth's store and bought pieces for a crib scene, which we later assembled under the Christmas tree. My initial encounter with Jesus was with someone who was roughly my size and perhaps a little smaller. Parents and grandparents, aunts and uncles, also introduced me to religious practices—the Sign of the Cross, a prayer before bedtime, going to church, lighting a candle, taking holy water. I understand now that they placed me in this symbolic world and did so with little explanation. It became, however, a familiar world in which I was comfortable, a world that belonged to me as it belonged to my family.

My entrance into elementary school marked another phase in the journey. Somewhere in my brother's basement is a copy of my first religion textbook from first grade. It has a blue binding and contains pictures of the Garden of Eden, Moses, and scenes from the life of Jesus and Mary. I still have in my own possession another textbook, Father McGuire's *The New*

Baltimore Catechism and Mass—No. 2, Official Revised Edition. These books and the explanations of the Sisters who taught religion began a process of naming the content of faith, what we were called to believe. As I retrieve this early phase of my formation in faith, certain elements stand out in retrospect. The first element is the heavy dose of abstractions that had to be memorized but that still remained largely incomprehensible to me as a young child. These abstractions included concepts such as Supreme Being, creation, grace, sacrifice, and redemption. They became seeds for thought for another day. The second element of early religious formation was much livelier. It was a religious world populated by many people—Jesus and Mary, of course, but also many biblical characters, various saints, and finally the official religious people who lived here and now, our priests and Sisters. In some measure, these persons made up for the abstractions that we had to memorize. They embodied faith and made it attractive and challenging, something that might be in reach for me. The third and final element of my early religious formation was the unequivocal way in which faith was presented. Faith was not suggested, not offered as a choice among others, not a possibility that could be accepted or rejected. Faith was simply true, something that any sensible person would necessarily accept.

The Sisters who taught me, in whose hospital I was born, and to whom I am so deeply indebted belonged to the Congregation of the Poor Sisters of Saint Francis Seraph of Perpetual Adoration of Mishawaka, Indiana. The name was too long for us to remember or to say easily, and so we simply called them the Franciscan Sisters. They left Germany and arrived in the United States at the end of the nineteenth century, partly because of the stifling atmosphere of Bismarck's *Kulturkampf* for the Church's mission and ministry. They also came to serve significant needs in the Catholic community in this nation for education and health care.

The Sisters centered their educational efforts in faith formation. The kind of catechesis that they offered me continued the earlier trajectory of my journey toward faith. In other words, as my parents had done earlier, the Sisters brought me into in contact with the concepts and practices of faith without expecting that I would fully understand or appropriate their meaning immediately. In retrospect, it is clear to me that their method was prescriptive. They prescribed the behavior of faith: learn this, pray this, do this, do not do that. In skeletal form, they offered me what today we would identify as the four pillars of the *Catechism of the Catholic Church*: profession of faith, celebration of the Christian mystery, morality or life in Christ, and prayer or Christian spirituality.

From this description, it may seem that how the Sisters fostered faith was primarily a cognitive exercise. In fact, that is not true. They attended to the "feeling side" of faith, especially through their attention to the Eucharist and the sacrament of Penance. Because they were "Sisters of Perpetual Adoration," they encouraged a felt attachment to the Lord present in this sacrament. Because they carefully prepared us for confession or the sacrament of Penance, they communicated the important consequences—for good or for ill—that our decisions and actions had. This had little or nothing to do with the largely meaningless shibboleth of "Catholic guilt." It had everything to do with becoming a responsible human being.

Although the Sisters mainly taught in a prescriptive way, the affective or feeling dimension that they also underscored was moving us toward a more personal faith. Things were building within me, even though I had no conscious awareness of that. And then this journey to personal faith became a journey into faith. For me, an unexpected breakthrough moment occurred in fourth grade.

One day, one of the parish priests, Father Keenan, came to our classroom. I remember that he always had good stories and put a different, unexpected spin on the teaching that he offered us. This day, he said something quite simple, which, in retrospect and with my own years of experience as a priest, I would identify as a very deep part of his own personal experience. He told us how good God had been to us, how blessed we were, how we must never forget that. Translated in language that I later acquired, he told us that we were living in a world of grace and that the only adequate response to that fact was constant gratitude.

I must have heard something like that before, but this time it struck me deeply. I have never forgotten it. Up to that point, I had been brought to faith, brought to Baptism, and brought to the concepts and practices of faith. From that moment on, I brought myself to faith. This was the moment in which I consciously and freely accepted the Good News.

These initial and early moments of my faith history correspond to the larger movements of history and community that I considered earlier. I received Baptism and the summons to faith because from generation to generation the Church, entrusted with the Word of life, continued to share the mystery of Jesus Christ until it arrived in my own life. The Second Vatican Council's "Dogmatic Constitution on Divine Revelation" states, "God graciously arranged that the things he had once revealed for the salvation of all peoples should remain in their

entirety, throughout the ages, and be transmitted to all generations"
(*Dei Verbum*, 7).

Well before I began to understand the personal summons of
faith and make it my own, I belonged to the faith of the Church. My
personal journey, from its very beginnings, has never been a solitary
enterprise. I have been in the company of others. And this is the way
salvation comes into this world. "God has ... willed to make men holy
and save them, not as individuals without any bond or link between
them, but rather to make them into a people who might acknowledge
him and serve him in holiness" (*Lumen Gentium*, 9). The faith of the
Church that brought me to my faith was no abstraction. It had the face
of my parents, grandparents, and godparents, the face of the priests
who celebrated sacraments, and the face of the Sisters who taught me.

My faith was a grace and a gift from its very beginning. When I
was brought to Baptism as an infant, I had not asked for the sacrament,
and I had not earned it or deserved it. I was brought to Baptism, the
sacrament of faith and the gateway to faith, as a sheer gift from the
goodness of God and the people who loved me. The words of St. Paul
were taking root in me and describing my situation:

> The righteousness of God has been disclosed, and is attested by
> the law and the prophets, the righteousness of God through faith in
> Jesus Christ for all who believe. For there is no distinction, since all
> have sinned and fall short of the glory of God; they are now justified
> by his grace as a gift, through the redemption that is in Christ Jesus,
> whom God put forward as a sacrifice of atonement by his blood,
> effective through faith. (Rom 3:20–25a)

As I retrieve this early layer of my faith history, I perceive very
clearly how much faith comprehends the full range of human experience. Early on, I learned about faith, formed attachments based on faith,
and behaved in a certain way because of faith. This early experience

demonstrates how faith touches every significant dimension of being human. So, faith involves knowledge—knowing God's revelation and the ways of God—and it is, therefore, something cognitive. Faith also has to do with attachment. It has a feeling or affective side. And finally, faith has consequences for decisions and actions and, in general, for taking responsibility in this world. Faith shapes values and attitudes. Finally, although faith is certainly spiritual, that does not mean that it is immaterial. I arrived in the realm of faith through signs and gestures and language and people I could see and touch. Faith, like my very self, has spiritual and material dimensions.

My early history also belies the way that people categorize those who believe and those who do not believe. Often, they split humanity into two distinct groups, the believers and the unbelievers. That duality, however, does not capture the lived reality of faith. There is, in my experience and the experience of others, a more complex journey. I was coming to faith across the years. At first, as an infant, I was brought forward into a community of faith. Gradually, then, I developed foundations for personal faith in my capacity to trust and to be free. Later, I learned the realities that faith embraces, came to a deeper understanding of them, and eventually accepted them. In all of this, I can honestly say that I was not an unbeliever one moment and then a believer the next. I was coming to faith, in a way similar to that of many people in the gospels. As the Samaritans of the town of Sychar told their townswoman who had been at the well with Jesus: "It is no longer because of what you said that we believe, for we have heard for ourselves, and we know that this is truly the Savior of the world" (Jn 4:42). Or listen to Peter's words to Jesus after his Bread of Life discourse: "We have come to believe and know that you are the Holy One of God" (Jn 6:69). I came to believe. People generally come to believe. We journey, and we engage in a process that leads us to embrace the Word of life.

Finally, as I retrieve this early history of my journey of faith, I am fascinated by that moment in fourth grade when Father Keenan's words struck such a deep chord in my heart and awakened in a decisively new way my own personal faith. What exactly was happening here?

St. Augustine once spoke to his people about this experience. He told them that he was proclaiming God's word to them and that he did this by speaking an external word to them. He went on to say that only if God was drawing them interiorly to comprehend and accept this external word would it bear fruit in faith. One passage Augustine certainly had in mind was from John's gospel: "No one can come to me unless drawn by the Father" (Jn 6:44a). He could have also cited the Acts of the Apostles and the conversion of Lydia, the dealer in purple goods from the city of Thyatira. As Paul preached the Word of life and salvation, the text says, "[t]he Lord opened her heart to listen eagerly to what was said by Paul" (Acts 16:14b). This God-given capacity, an interior gift or grace, to be able to receive the word as the word of God and word of faith was in Paul's mind when he wrote to the Thessalonians: "We also constantly give thanks to God for this, that when you received the word of God that you heard from us, you accepted it not as a human word but as what it really is, God's word, which is also at work in you believers" (1 Thess 2:13).

Theologians have called this graced interior gift the *lumen fidei*, the "light of faith," or in more recent and technical theological language, "supernatural intentionality." Whatever the name, the experience tells us the external word meets the interior openness—and all this in the person. Faith truly comes as a gift. This fact also speaks to the futility or impossibility of "trying to think ourselves into faith," that is, reasoning our way toward believing. That does not mean that faith is irrational, only that it is not rational, even though—as we shall later see—it is eminently reasonable.

In that fourth-grade classroom, I can clearly affirm that there was something more than Father Keenan and his words, something more than my listening to him. Within me was a gift not of my own making that enabled me to receive another gift also not of my own making: the gift of personal and freely accepted faith.

What were the decisive moments of my coming to explicit faith? Who were the people who were instrumental in that process?

Chapter 13

CONSIDERED FAITH: STUDYING FAITH FOR UNDERSTANDING AND COMMUNICATION

The Necessary but Limited Task of Analyzing Faith

*A*s I matured into adolescence, faith continued to matter deeply to me. I experienced great fascination with the faith that I held within myself and with the faith that I saw in the Church and other believers. I was also curious. I had questions and, at times, struggles in trying to make sense of things. I continued to explore faith not only as something to be understood but also as something expressed, as something beautiful—as I found it, for example, in art and architecture and music. And in some inchoate way, I also understood faith as an instrument to change the world, something that could make all the difference for human relationships, for justice, peace, and reconciliation.

There were many things that I wanted to do and could have done with my life. In the flood of possibilities, I kept coming back to what seemed to matter most to me. It was faith; that one word that was shorthand for a rich and complex mix of my experience and aspirations. I decided to center my life on that. I entered the seminary, prepared for priesthood, eventually did graduate work in theology, and then taught and served as a priest in different contexts.

In this phase of retrieving an important layer of my faith, I must focus on my studies. The intellectual understanding of faith occupied many years of my life as a student and as a teacher. Although an intellectual approach to faith always remains partial and not necessarily the most important path of exploration, it responds to a powerful and significant human need for coherence. We are always unsettled, until we grasp how the most important dimensions of our lives fit together. For my own journey, the sense of a coherent vision of faith also provided a foundational layer for what has most recently become for me a fuller and deeper experience of faith. The years dedicated to the study of faith form an essential layer of my history.

This part of the story begins with the confident American Catholic world of my adolescence and early young adulthood in the 1950s and early '60s. There seemed to be a singular voice for faith that was consistent, unified, and clear. The Second Vatican Council was beginning and gaining momentum. For those who followed the early years of the Council, it did not signal changes in the faith or, even more radically, of faith. As it began, the Council was about what the Italians call *perfezionamento*, greater competency or greater proficiency to carry on the Church's mission in the world. And that explained Pope John XXIII's call for *aggiornamento* or updating.

Then, in 1966, a year after the Council concluded, I went to Rome to begin my theological studies at the Gregorian University. In Europe, I discovered an entirely different world that seemed largely in disarray, especially in contrast to what I had previously experienced. Inside and outside the classroom, the dominant climate was adversarial. As the Roman graffiti splashed on walls all over the city described it, everything was a *lotta continua*, a struggle that just kept going on and on.

In the context of understanding faith, who exactly were the adversaries? In the classroom, a key adversary was the specter of nineteenth-century rationalism, reducing all knowledge to what we could reason to, as well as its twentieth-century manifestation in scientism, affirming only truths that were scientifically and empirically verifiable. This mentality had entered the Church itself at the beginning of the twentieth century in the form of Modernism, a way of thinking that re-aligned revelation and faith to conform to rationalist and scientific thought. Another adversary was the alternate spiritual vision of Marxism that sought to create heaven on earth with human effort alone and to ride to that victory on the steam of human conflict. A less obvious and stealthier adversary was a growing and indifferent secular climate fueled by capitalism unanchored to human values and all too ready to tolerate inequity and injustice for the sake of profit. Another emergent adversary was a sclerotic cultural Catholicism, especially in Europe at that time, a religiosity that depended on convention and lacked believers with real and robust commitment. Finally, in the wake of the Council, adversaries seemed to be living in the very same house of the Church. On one side were strident calls for radical reform of faith and Church; on the other was a fervent insistence on reclaiming the true faith of the past and on re-entrenchment.

At twenty-two years old and with what I felt to be a strong and determined faith, I now walked into a maelstrom.

The four years of preliminary theological studies and the subsequent three years of doctoral work were not simple. In fact, at times they were excruciatingly painful, as I tried to navigate the currents that pulled me in many different directions while I tried to maintain a hold on the integrity of faith while also trying to understand it more deeply. In the turmoil, God was good. By his grace, I had great teachers at the Gregorian University. They had their limitations and could not resolve every issue I was encountering, but they provided the essential foundations that enabled me to move forward. In fact, after my own years of teaching, I look back and can recognize in my teachers their strength of intellect and conviction that were tested in the crucible of those turbulent years.

It would be impossible and tedious to summarize seven years of studying faith. I can, however, identify two clusters of teaching that gave me the navigational capacity that I so needed at the time and that have continued to serve me even now. The first cluster led me to understand the nature of faith; the second led me to understand the experience of faith.

Father Juan Alfaro, S.J., taught a course on faith. He began with biblical foundations, named developments across history, and focused in a more concentrated way on the relevant contemporary issues concerning faith. His 650-page text *Fides, Spes, Caritas* is a formidable exposition in Latin mainly of faith, but it also includes some treatment of hope and charity—the three theological virtues. I cannot distill all his teaching, but I can share essential pieces that contributed to my journey of understanding faith in general and my own faith more particularly. I can identify six points of teaching that Father Alfaro provided for an essential understanding of faith, based on his *Fides, Spes, Caritas*. [1]

Echoing the First Vatican Council, Alfaro insisted that believing is a reasonable decision. The word "reasonable" deserves some special attention. Faith is not rational. The act of faith is not the end product of a reasoning process, which involves summoning the data, processing it in our own heads, and then coming to a reasoned conclusion based on the evidence. Faith is not rational in that sense. Faith, on the other hand, is indeed reasonable. The act of faith is coherent with human intelligence and right reasoning. To assent to the truth of faith and to trust God, even if that faith is not just based on empirical evidence, is a reasonable and human act.

Alfaro also taught that faith has a secure foundation in the human spirit. Faith corresponds to the deepest human longings and aspirations. Embedded within us is an infinite outreach for truth and love, an infinite outreach that can only be satisfied by infinity—by God, who is the fullness of being.

These human dimensions of faith led Alfaro to a third truth of faith. In the act of believing, faith is and must be free. If faith depended on evidence, we would be compelled by the evidence to believe. As it is, faith comes to us as a free invitation to believe and to trust. God does not compel us. Everything about authentic faith speaks of respect for our freedom.

In its truest sense, this faith that is human and free comes to us as God's gift. It belongs to us, but it comes to us as a grace. Faith is never earned, deserved, or merited. And that gift of faith links us to the great gift and single center of faith—our salvation in Jesus Christ. Faith may move us in many directions, but it points us to one center, our salvation in Christ.

Our faith belongs to our life on earth, and Father Alfaro never tired of telling us that, in this state, faith is always bound to be incomplete. Our final destiny moves us beyond faith and enables us to enter the very presence of God and see God face-to-face. Our destiny is the vision of God, and faith is what brings us to that destiny. Believers are pilgrims, on the way, not yet arrived, who hope that one day by God's grace they will arrive. For that reason, faith always makes us aware of the incompleteness of our life as it is.

The understanding that I received in studying faith with Father Alfaro has served me well. To know faith as reasonable, human, free, a gift, centered in Christ, and leading us beyond our present experience—this has enable me to appreciate faith in itself for my own journey, to sort through and analyze the countless (and often incomplete or incorrect) presentations of faith in today's world, and, finally, to help believers in the Church understand what they believe and how they believe.

After my four years of general theological studies in preparation for ordination to the priesthood, I began a specialized doctoral program in the Gregorian University's Institute of Spirituality. These studies in spirituality took me in a different direction in my exploration of faith. The earlier years and especially the teaching of Juan Alfaro focused my attention on the cognitive and analytical aspects of faith. In contrast, the study of spirituality probed ways to understand the Christian experience and means to foster it or develop it. In the study of Christian spirituality, I revisited faith—but now from an experiential and practical perspective.

The first and perhaps one of the most significant challenges of this phase of my studies was to grasp the word and concept of "experience." Everyone seems to know what experience means, and they use the word freely. Ask someone to explain it, however, and you will probably draw a blank look. If knowing and promoting "the Christian experience" is the task of spirituality, then it is critical to have a clear understanding of what the Christian experience means.

I came to understand that human experience has to do with what makes us distinctively human—our cognition, our feelings, and our values. Cognition includes how we perceive the world around us and how we understand it. Feelings are not just transitory states of emotion but pathways of connection and relationship. Values, what we hold dear, shape attitudes and lead us to make decisions and take action.

Our most deeply significant relationships shape our human experience, as cognition, feelings, and values. For example, this is the case in a parent-child relationship. Parents' relationships with their children shape their cognition, their feelings, and their values. Parents perceive and understand the world differently—for example, as a place for playing and a place where danger lurks for a toddler. Parents feel and connect differently with others, such as when they read news stories about teenagers like their own caught in spirals of violence. They can be empathic with others and identify with them because of their own parent-child relationship. Parents also cultivate certain values and make decisions because of their relationship with their children—for example, saving money for future educational expenses. The relationship does indeed shape the human experience in all its dimensions.

It is a short step to linking our experience of God in faith with the same pattern. The relationship with God in faith shapes our human experience. Because of the relationship in faith, we find ourselves perceiving the world and other people differently. Is that not the point of Jesus' parables, such as that of the Good Samaritan? Because of the relationship in faith, we find ourselves feeling differently and relating differently to others—for example, in compassion with the least of our brothers and sisters, or in forgiveness with our enemies. Because of the relationship in faith, we find ourselves valuing things differently, making decisions about material things and life directions that others may find difficult to understand.

That experiential study of faith in spirituality led me to the Bible, the history of the saints, the relationship of psychology and faith, and the struggles of ordinary believers trying to make their way in this world.

This layer of my life history, stretched across the years studying theology and spirituality and then teaching it for some time, constitutes a very important part of my faith journey. Although much of this study and teaching centered on an intellectual and analytical approach to faith, there was also room to explore the direct experience of faith. And this opportunity has been decisive across the past four decades of my life.

Initially, this part of my journey of faith, the journey of understanding, seems clear and self-contained and very much in the realm of ideas. Early on and even today, I remain committed to St. Anselm's description of theology as *fides quaerens intellectum*, "faith seeking understanding." There is truth in this assessment, but there is also more.

Understanding the link between human experience and faith experience began in other layers of my history—for example, in the influence of St. Francis of Assisi, who retrieved a vivid sense of the humanity of Jesus and the realism of the Incarnation. And this understanding leads us beyond the realm of intellect into the very heart and intention of God. To know the link between the human and the divine in faith is to know how God acts toward us. God comes to us on our terms, in the way of humanity, when he comes among us as the Word made flesh. That conviction about the Incarnation puts faith at the center of life, of human life, of my life.

The understanding that faith is a human choice, a free and human assent, a human movement in line with our deepest aspirations for knowledge and love, as well as a gift that takes hold of us in our humanity—all this is important in itself. It is also a powerful corrective to very misguided and incorrect assessments of faith. Some contemporary voices decry religious faith as dehumanizing, as a source of violence and mistrust. Others coming from religious fundamentalism rob faith of its humanity with terrible consequences. For them, there is no freedom, no connection with what is best in us, and no divine gift taking hold and transforming our humanity.

An important passage from the First Letter of John locates faith in the experience of humanity: "By this you know the Spirit of God: every spirit that confesses that Jesus Christ has come in the flesh is from God, and every spirit that does not confess Jesus is not from God" (1 Jn 4:2–3). Confessing the mystery of faith in the reality of humanity and divinity coming together in the Word made flesh—that is the standard of true faith.

My own journey of understanding, at least for the period that I described, took a distinctively intellectual and conceptual direction. It is critically important—as I later reflect on this period—to note that this conceptual understanding did open outward to a much larger horizon, as I will describe it. An intellectual understanding of faith also carries its own inherent limitations. If faith involves an absolutely deep relationship of human and divine intimacy, then the experienced relationship with God will always outpace our ability to understand it and explain it. We remain unable to explain our deepest human relationships. How could we then imagine thoroughly explaining and expressing our relationship with God? More to the point is Pascal's observation, "The heart has its reasons that reason does not know." Blessed John Henry Cardinal

Newman similarly, in speaking of faith, said that everyone has a reason for believing, but not everyone can articulate that reason. In faith, we stand before mystery—indeed, are immersed in mystery.[2] In the course of my ministry over these past four decades, the intellectual understanding of faith has opened toward a wider horizon.

When I have wanted to understand my faith?
What resources have I found helpful?

Chapter 14

TRANSFORMED AND TRANSFORMING FAITH

Faith beyond Doctrine, Devotion, and Morality

*T*he final piece of my faith history covers my last forty-four years as a priest. Unlike the other layers of history, with their specific points of closure, this one is still active and in formation.

When I speak of my public ministry as a priest and my personal history of faith, I am bridging two inextricably linked movements. As a priest, I have served faith in the lives of other people, but their journeys of faith have served and transformed my own journey of faith as well. Whether people gave witness to an extraordinary and authentic faith or even to a very much misconstrued sense of faith, their journey—usually unknown to them—became intertwined with my own.

Because of these linked movements of faith, I call myself a priest-participant in the faith journeys of those whom I have served. Again, in this position, I have both given something and have also received something, usually much more—in my estimation—than I have given. I have been challenged, chastened, and uplifted—sometimes all at once.

Let me begin with the experience of true or genuine faith that I have found in the lives of those whom I have served. Perhaps the phrase "true faith" raises a question. How do we know true faith in someone when we see it? In my experience, people manifest true faith in three ways—in their knowledge of God, in the trust they place in God, and in the difference that faith has made in their lives.

When I encounter someone who knows God and knows the ways of God very clearly, I detect true faith. I am not speaking of theological knowledge or sophisticated expressions of belief. I am thinking of people whose words echo to me what I find in the Gospel. They know that God is provident, just, merciful, and—above all—loving. There is nothing fancy in this knowledge. They simply know who God is, how God acts, and what the ways of God are.

In addition to knowing God, people of true faith have a deep trust and confidence in God. This trust and confidence does not waver with the winds of prosperity or adversity. It is both steady and deep. They express this trust when they describe the direction of their lives, especially when they encounter painful limits, such as physical illness or the disappointing behavior of others.

Finally, a third sign of true faith is the difference that faith makes. Without faith, the lives of these true believers would be unimaginable. You cannot explain who they are, why they feel the way they do, and how they make the decisions they make except for the reason that they really and truly believe in God. In my experience as a priest, when I have found knowledge, trust, and difference in people, I am confident that I am encountering persons of true faith. And those encounters have had a deep and lasting impact on me.

Across forty-four years, I have had many positive and even transformative encounters with people of faith. Obviously, I cannot give an account of all of them, but I can offer some examples. One extraordinary encounter came at the very beginning of my ministry shortly after ordination.

On weekends, I celebrated Mass and visited patients at Carlo Forlanini Hospital in Rome, a public hospital that cared mainly for poor people who came from various parts of central and southern Italy. I covered a department that specialized in those suffering from tuberculosis of the bone. I did not understand the medical condition very well except through the bits and pieces that nurses and patients communicated to me. Many patients were hospitalized for very long periods of time and immobilized with body casts. Some indicated that their problems were either caused or aggravated by previous medical care that had been of poor quality. Because of the pain, the discomfort of treatments, and the separation from family, it was easy to understand how the patients and staff caring for them felt deeply challenged. Still, in this grim environment, I found resilient and extraordinary experiences of faith. This left its mark on me as a young priest, and it has never left me.

One patient, for example, had been hospitalized almost continuously for seven years. He was a relatively young married man with a family and was from a small provincial town. Most of his days were spent immobilized in bed. He read and did puzzles. He prayed. When he spoke to me of his condition and of his sense of God, I was completely amazed. No word of sadness, no word of anger or bitterness, came from him. He was completely at peace. Although he was very unsophisticated and not highly educated, he articulated a confident trust and hope in God that was astounding. I had years of theological training and had recently been ordained a priest, but I knew that I was in the presence of someone well beyond me in their depth and expanse of faith.

On that same floor were three religious Sisters who were also the nurse-managers for this section of the hospital. They were completely dedicated to their work. In effect they never left their work, because they lived nearby. They manifested their faith in absorbing, mediating, and reconciling the often discordant voices and feelings of those they served: the attending physicians with big egos and short patience, the nurses and orderlies of varying levels of dependability, and the patients with their personal complaints and frequent interpersonal scuffles. These women radiated faith and determination. Their faith belonged to God, and there was no doubt about that as they spoke to me of their prayer. At the same time, their faith clearly directed what they did for others. It was extraordinarily practical and lived out in this world as it is. Again, I understood myself to be in the presence of people who had unlocked the implications of faith in a way that I was just beginning to understand.

Across the years of priesthood, many other people echoed the faith experiences that I first encountered in Carlo Forlanini Hospital. Some of these drew from their faith in the midst of significant struggles with sickness, terminal illness, sudden loss, unemployment, troubled marriages, emotional difficulties, and broken relationships. Others, such as the Sisters at Carlo Forlanini Hospital, lived lives of great dedication inspired by their faith. Among these were loving and self-sacrificing married couples, seminarians, priests, religious, lay ministers, and many "ordinary" but, indeed, extraordinary believers.

There is another group of true believers who have opened up new perspectives for my own journey of faith. They are young children and developmentally disabled young people and adults. In these groups, there is obviously little articulation of faith. Rather, they are caught up in an immediate experience of joyful appreciation of God.

At different points in my priesthood, I have prepared young children for the sacraments of Reconciliation and first Eucharist. These moments have amazed me and changed me. Generally, I sit with them—in one of their classroom chairs if it will accommodate me—and hold a conversation with them. My task is to inform them and, even more, to encourage them. They have always been very willing and very enthusiastic. I have detected their joyful appreciation of God, who wants to come close to them and to be with them. Intuitively and in faith, they know this and receive it joyfully. The immediacy and directness of their experience along with its lack of verbiage have led me to understand the prayer that we identify as contemplation and even some essential elements of mysticism. My conversations with these children have had a purifying effect on my faith, and I am led to greater simplicity.

The extraordinary witness of people who truly believed and lived from their faith has given my own faith new life and renewal. At the same time, less positive experiences of others' faith have yielded some important benefits. Even when I encountered people whose faith seemed incomplete or even distorted, I found a challenge that pushed me deeper into the meaning of faith.

For example, a major distortion of faith that I have found among some people is the reduction of faith to one of its dimensions. This might mean reducing faith to adherence to doctrines and so identifying faith exclusively with *what is believed.* It is also possible to reduce faith to the practices of religion and devotion, in other words, to *outward practices meant to express and support faith.* Finally, faith can be reduced to a set of moral standards or *single-mindedly attempting to do the right thing.* In fact, each of these dimensions of faith—doctrine, devotion, morality—has validity and reflects an essential dimension of faith. When one of these dimensions, however, becomes the dominant and defining feature of faith, then faith itself can be reduced to dogmatism or devotionalism or moralism. And in that reduction, the fullness of faith is lost along with its heart: a living relationship with the living God.

We are all susceptible to these reductions and distortions of the fullness of faith. Clearly, it is easier to manage what I believe, how I engage religious practices, or how I evaluate right and wrong, than to enter into the intimate and sometimes complicated relationship with God that true and full faith signals.

When I have encountered people who embrace a reduced faith—whether doctrinal, devotional, or moral—I find myself challenged both personally as a believer and ministerially as a priest.

The personal challenge rests in the honest recognition of my own propensity to reduce faith to a simpler and less complicated dimension. That is a temptation that I must resist through a process of honest self-scrutiny. The reduced faith I detect in others reminds me of my own challenge to embrace faith more fully.

The ministerial challenge for me is to determine the best way to help people who are stuck in a reduced faith that clings to one dimension and so becomes dogmatism, devotionalism, or moralism. It is a challenge to know how to invite people who are lopsidedly preoccupied with what they believe, or with how they engage religious practices, or with figuring out the right thing to do. In striving to meet these ministerial challenges, theology can be helpful, but in itself it is insufficient. Theology offers conceptual clarity and a theoretical framework. That is valuable but limited. In helping people to expand their sense of faith, the direct faith experiences of the saints seem to me to be far more effective, because their experiences move beyond concepts and theory to demonstrate an integral life of faith in its many dimensions.

In my own personal and ministerial journey, I have drawn in a particular way from the faith experience of three saintly women—Teresa of Jesus, Thérèse of Lisieux, and Mother Teresa of Calcutta. Each one's experience breaks open an expanded vision of faith and summons us to embrace a larger and more integral sense of believing. In matters of faith, the saints are our true and reliable teachers.

Teresa of Jesus and Reaching the
Person beyond the Doctrine

The life and spiritual experience of Teresa of Jesus verify an extraordinarily important observation about the nature of faith made by St. Thomas Aquinas. He wrote: *"Actus credentis non terminatur ad enuntiabile sed ad rem,"* "The act of a believing person does not end in a statement of belief but in the reality affirmed in that statement."[1]

Thomas Aquinas affirms that faith carries us through doctrine, ultimately to the very reality that the doctrine affirms. In other words, faith brings us into relationship with God. Faith, then, is not reducible to a statement or some information about God. Faith's destination is entrance into that sublime relationship that, in fact, eludes full and precise conceptualization and verbalization.

At different points, Teresa's orthodoxy was suspect and the object of investigation by the Spanish Inquisition. In fact, these suspicions arose because of spiritual movements in the Spain of her day that exaggerated various forms of direct experience of God. Teresa professed the orthodox faith of the Church and submitted to the Church's authority. Her faith and her experience of faith moved her to embrace and more directly experience the reality that she acknowledged when she professed her faith. The *Book of Her Life* abounds with examples of her faith leading her to experience her relationship with God.

One example has to do with her faith in the incarnate Word. She affirms the doctrine and reality of the Incarnation, and by God's grace she is moved to embrace the reality she professes in her living relationship with Jesus Christ by way of his humanity. She writes:

> The Lord helps us, strengthens us, and never fails; He is a true friend. And I see clearly, and I saw afterward, that God desires that if we are going to please Him and receive His great favors, we must do so through the most sacred humanity of Christ, in whom He takes His delight. Many, many times have I perceived this truth through experience. The Lord has told it to me. I have definitely seen that we must enter by this gate if we desire His sovereign Majesty to show us great secrets.[2]

Notice that she says, "I perceived this truth through experience." The truth perceived and professed is the same truth experienced as the reality of her relationship with Jesus Christ through his humanity.

In another passage, Teresa describes her experience of prayer. She says: "I trust then in the mercy of God, who never fails to repay anyone who has taken Him for a friend. For mental prayer in my opinion is nothing else than an intimate sharing between friends; it means taking time frequently to be alone with Him who we know loves us."[3]

Again, she begins with faith. She professes the existence of God, but that affirmation, that "enunciable" in the language of Thomas Aquinas, is not the endpoint of her faith. She moves in faith to embrace her relationship with God as intimate friend in her prayer.

The doctrine of faith is absolutely critical for Teresa and for us. Doctrine must be true, and it must be precise and solid. This is so, not because of doctrine's value in itself. Rather, doctrine bridges the individual believer into the reality of relationship with God. That bridge, then, must be solid and reliable. At the same time, it is essential to remember that it is a bridge, that it serves a purpose beyond itself.

Teresa of Jesus has helped me to understand faith's affirmations, its doctrine, and the larger direction that doctrine takes us: into the very reality of relationship with God. An occupational hazard for me as a theologian and as a priest of the Church is to lock onto the enunciables or statements of faith without sufficient recognition that their truth and validity depend on leading us to relationship with the divine reality. In these last dozen or so years, I hear myself preaching differently. I am less expository, less explanatory, and probably—much for the better—less clever. Through my words, I am now trying to push my listeners and myself beyond the words. Words can reflect, but they can never embody or encapsulate the reality of the holy mystery of God, who calls us to intimate union. Teresa of Jesus, this first muse of faith, has taught me and continues to teach me.

Thérèse of Lisieux and Reaching Union beyond Feelings

Thérèse of Lisieux died in 1897 at the age of twenty-four. Nine years earlier she had entered the Carmel of Lisieux, where she lived a life of prayer and dedication in her community of Sisters. Her autobiography abounds with experiences of devotion and deep feelings of confidence in God and in the heavenly future that God was preparing for her.

When she was twenty-three, she became ill with tuberculosis. In the last year of her life, the shape of her faith journey and spiritual life shifted in a very different direction. She shares this part of her journey in her autobiography, *The Story of a Soul*. She writes:

At this time [that is, up to the time of her illness] I was enjoying such a living faith, such a clear faith, that I was unable to believe that there were really impious people who had no faith. I believed they were actually speaking against their own inner convictions when they denied the existence of heaven, that beautiful heaven where God Himself wanted to be their Eternal Reward. During those very joyful days of the Easter season, Jesus made me feel that there were really souls who have no faith, and who, through the abuse of grace, lost this precious treasure, the source of the only real and pure joys. He permitted my soul to be invaded by the thicket darkness, and that the thought of heaven, up until then so sweet to me, be no longer anything but the cause of struggle and torment. This trial was to last not a few days or a few weeks, it was not to be extinguished until the hour set by God Himself and this hour has not yet come. I would like to be able to express what I feel, but alas! I believe this is impossible. One would have to travel through this dark tunnel to understand its darkness.[4]

Amazingly, in this trial of faith, Thérèse did not retreat from her relationship with God in Jesus Christ. In fact, the exact opposite happened. She drew even closer in faith to Jesus, just as she felt his absence.

So, she writes: "Ah! May Jesus pardon me if I have caused Him any pain, but He knows very well that while I do not have the joy of faith, I am trying to carry out its works at least. I believe I have made more acts of faith in this past year than all through my whole life.... I run towards my Jesus. I tell Him I am ready to shed my blood to the last drop to profess my faith in the existence of heaven."[5]

When she was at the moment of death, her very last words were: "Oh! I love Him!" and a moment later, "My God, I love you."[6]

What happened in Thérèse's experience is extraordinary in itself, but, even more, it casts new and surprising light on the nature of faith itself.

The teaching of the Church, for example, affirms that faith is absolutely certain. The *Catechism of the Catholic Church* says: "Faith is more certain than all human knowledge because it is founded on the very word of God who cannot lie" (CCC, 157). For those who have questions and struggles concerning faith—and I include myself among them—it is difficult to understand how faith can be absolutely certain and how it has no room for doubt. The experience of Thérèse breaks through this impasse. The joy of faith and a confident sense of heaven would both bespeak a sense of certitude, but she has neither joy nor a clear sense of heaven's reality. The certitude that she does have is the absolutely unshakable reality of her relationship of love with Jesus, her love for him and his love for her. She knows the relationship and is absolutely certain about it. There is no proof of the relationship or the love, because both the relationship and the love attached to it are self-validating. Yet, it is clear, and it is certain. It is almost as if Thérèse could face the prospect of no afterlife and no heaven but resolutely and absolutely cling to the reality of Jesus and his love as the one important and enduring thing. Thérèse has led me to claim faith's certitude in no uncertain terms.

Another light that she offers me concerns the place of the mediations of religion and devotion in faith. In her earlier journey of faith, Thérèse had a positive experience of these mediations of religion and devotion. I mean that her participation in the sacraments of the Church, various forms of devotion, and personal prayer all mediated a faith experience of the presence of God. In and through faith, she sensed or felt the relationship with God. Now, in the last year of her life, what mediated her relationship with God in faith fell away. And here is the great paradox of her faith. The absence of the mediations of religion and devotion with their accompanying feelings did not diminish her faith relationship with God but rather intensified it and made it more immediate. There is less "between" Thérèse and Jesus, which leads to the deepened immediacy of her relationship. From another perspective, the paradox is her experience of the presence of God in God's felt absence. And from yet another perspective, the paradox is her most intense experience of union with Jesus precisely in her most intense feeling of solitude and abandonment.

I stand before Thérèse of Lisieux's experience in amazement. Her path of faith led her to entrust herself without qualification or reserve. The poverty of her dark night in her trial of faith was absolute. I have glimpsed her experience in my own journey of faith, but only in very partial and halting ways. I have not fully embraced her path of complete self-emptying surrender. With God's grace, that may be ahead on my journey before I die.

In my accompaniment of others, in my service to the world, and in my own continuing journey of faith before that final surrender, the legacy of Thérèse's journey of faith has served me and continues to serve me well. She seems to belong so much to our world and our time. As our contemporary, she and her trajectory of faith challenge us to the very core of our being. She pushes us to radical detachment, which is the necessary prelude to radical union with God.

In the Church, with its countless holy resources of liturgy and devotional life, Thérèse instructs us not to make any practice of religion or devotion absolute. In a culture bent on stirring and fostering feelings to match relationships, Thérèse urges detachment of the feelings of faith from faith itself. In a time of material abundance that would seem to provide assurances of security, Thérèse points to poverty as the way to safety. In a world that prizes the control of life through science and technology, Thérèse summons us to surrender. In a century of worldwide violence and pain that seems to shout the absence of God, Thérèse charts a path for us to find the presence of God in God's sensed absence. I am daily challenged and encouraged by my prophetic muse of faith for today, St Thérèse of Lisieux.

Mother Teresa of Calcutta and Reaching the Way of Abundant Compassion beyond a Merely Dutiful Life

Mother Teresa of Calcutta died in 1997. She left a rich legacy to the world that included a path of compassion for the most abject and neediest people dwelling on this earth. She never let us forget the abandoned and dying poor and those struggling with illnesses, such as AIDS and Hansen's disease (leprosy). She nurtured the youngest and most vulnerable among us, and she cared for the elderly. She addressed people in the developed world who seemed to be materially well-off but who were desperately poor in life's most essential element, love.

Mother Teresa, who is best known for her charitable works, has helped me to understand a particular dimension of faith that is so susceptible to distortion. Before sharing that particular dimension, however, I feel that it is important to say a word about her overall journey of faith. That journey, like the one of Thérèse of Lisieux but in an even more protracted way, was a journey in darkness. Her journey in darkness surprises and shocks people who assume that her faith gave her a vibrant and immediate sense of the presence of God. In fact, the opposite was true. Once, when she was writing to a bishop in India, she said: "I want to say to you something—but I do not know how to express it. I am longing—with a painful longing to be all for God—to be holy in such a way that Jesus can live His life to the full in me. The more I want Him—the less I am wanted—I want to love Him as He has not been loved—and yet there is that separation—that terrible emptiness, that feeling of absence of God."[7]

Later, she offered an account of her spiritual journey to a priest who served her as a theological consultant and spiritual resource. She says:

> Darkness is such that I really do not see—neither with my mind nor with my reason.—The place of God in my soul is blank.—There is no God in me.... My very life seems so contradictory. I help souls—to go where?—Why all this? ...Yet deep down somewhere in my heart that longing for God keeps breaking through the darkness. When outside—in the work—or meeting people—there is a presence—of somebody living very close—in very me.—I don't know what this is—but very often even every day—that love in me for God grows more real.—I find myself telling Jesus unconsciously [what] most strange tokens of love. [8]

Mother Teresa's journey of faith was a walk in darkness, and her experience of God was more one of absence than of presence. And yet there was light, when she was "in the work," that is, bringing her compassionate care to the neediest. In her compassionate love for others, God's presence was mysteriously awakened. A particular light that Mother Teresa brings to my understanding of faith is her lived experience that unites faith and love. Her very life echoes the words of the First Letter of John: "And this is his commandment, that we should believe in the name of his Son Jesus Christ and love one another, just as he has commanded us" (1 Jn 3:23). Believing and loving, the verse tells us, go together.

Mother Teresa's commitment to compassion and love became the expression and practice of her faith. This commitment resulted from a call she heard from God at a very precise moment in her life. In 1946 while she was traveling on a train to a retreat in Darjeeling, she received a call to which she responded positively. She describes that moment in these words:

> [It] was a call within my vocation. It was a second calling. It was a vocation to give up even Loreto where I was very happy and to go out in the streets to serve the poorest of the poor. It was in that train, I heard the call to give up all and follow Him into the slums—to serve Him in the poorest of the poor. . . . I knew it was His will and that I had to follow Him. There was no doubt that it was going to be His work.[9]

The next year, as she relates it, she imagined in her prayer the call coming to her from those whom she would serve. She writes: "I saw a very big crowd—all kinds of people—very poor and children were there also. They all had their hands lifted toward me—standing in their midst. They called out 'Come, come, save us—bring us to Jesus.'"[10]

What is this particular light that Mother Teresa brings to faith for me and, indeed, for all of us? For many people who identify themselves as believers, faith is a matter of doing the right thing. Faith has to do primarily with doing good, being good, and avoiding evil. In an even more concentrated way, faith for them essentially entails the observance and fulfillment of rules and regulations. In other words, faith is equivalently a kind of moralism, a drive to do the right thing. Although this moralizing vision of faith belongs to many believers, it is also widely shared by those outside religion who only hear the Church making public pronouncements on moral issues.

I recognize in my own journey of faith my susceptibility to this moralizing brand of faith. I want to do good, and I want to be good. I want to be found righteous before God and other people. The problem here is not with morality. Indeed, there is good that ought to be embraced and evil that ought to be resisted or avoided. The problem is rather with the way that a moralizing framework for faith easily feeds egocentricity. Instead of faith as the journey into relationship with God, faith becomes a trajectory of my self-improvement, my self-enhancement, and—most sadly—my self-justification.

Mother Teresa's dark journey of faith lived out in loving compassion for others breaks the trap of egocentricity latent in a moralizing form of faith. At the same time, loving compassion, in fact, directs us on a genuine moral path of proper decisions and actions. Out of loving compassion born of faith come a sense of reverence for God and the fulfillment of the first three commandments of the Decalogue. Out of loving compassion born of faith also comes a profound respect for ourselves and others that enables us to observe the other commandments of the Decalogue as well as the Beatitudes and the works of mercy in our relationships with others.

Paradoxically, Mother Teresa has helped me to surrender my attachment to being a good person. For very long, I have thought that as a believer I needed to be a good person in my own eyes, in the eyes of others, and in God's eyes. I am beginning to see things differently with this third muse of my faith. In the measure I make myself available to God in faith and trust, even in the darkness, I will find myself embracing a path of compassionate love for others. Faith will free me from the shackles of my egocentricity. In the exercise of that love, I will find the right ways to live in reverence, respect, purity, justice, truth, and integrity of heart. All this is rooted in faith, but not the moralizing kind. It is the faith of rebirth that manifests itself in loving the other children of God: "Everyone who believes that Jesus is the Christ has been born of God, and everyone who loves the parent loves the child. By this we know that we love the children of God, when we love God and obey his commandments" (1 Jn 5:1–2).

How can saints I have known help me to understand my faith, purify it, and live it more genuinely?

Chapter 15

ELEMENTS OF AN AGENDA FOR THE CONTINUING JOURNEY OF FAITH

Faith beyond Chance, Death, and Institutions

I have gathered the layers of history that contributed to my journey of faith. The layers stretch back very far. Although I have not given all these historical pieces the deep and thorough attention they deserve, I feel that I have identified essential elements that have contributed to shaping my faith. Since I have not completed this journey of faith, more remains, and I am very conscious of that fact. Just as various challenges have shaped the past, so will challenges shape the future. And some of these challenges are already taking form. Three elements in particular will be, in my estimation, critical for the forward movement of my journey: (1) living with life as a free fall that also enjoys providential guidance; (2) peacefully appreciating the necessity of religion and Church for faith, even and especially when they are marred by limited and sinful humanity; and finally, (3) growing old and growing poor in order to come to an end.

Free Fall and Providence

The philosopher Martin Heidegger speaks of *Geworfenheit* or "thrownness" as characteristic of our existence. Without our free choice, we find ourselves in this world. In that sense, he suggests that we are "thrown" into existence. Beyond Heidegger's use of the term, I would suggest that much of life is thrown. Things happen for good or ill. I am more conscious of this when things do not go well. An accident, an illness, a natural disaster, an unleashing of random and destructive violence visited on innocent people—all this suggests thrownness or a state of free fall. According to physics, a free-falling object falls under the sole influence of gravity. No other forces direct or manage it. It just falls. In the same way, in life, it seems that things just happen. A more general sense of free fall pervades our existence overall.

Of course, to assert that all life and all existence is pure *Geworfenheit*, or free fall, counters a very basic premise of faith, namely, that the world and our existence in particular are guided by God's providential care. To affirm pure thrownness may be more radically antithetical to faith than denying some form of divine intelligent design in the evolution of the universe.

Here is the challenge to my faith. I experience this form of free fall or thrownness in life. In many ways, I have been shielded from the worst of it. If I lived in a different part of the world or in a different historical period, I would probably be facing it head on and daily. I anticipate some serious illness ahead. It usually happens before death. I anticipate some significant losses ahead. It usually happens if you live long enough. The pieces, I anticipate, will not hold together. I mean that these diminishments make life not only a matter of

chance but something incoherent. I anticipate *Geworfenheit*. At
the very same time, in faith and in my experience, I also have
an abiding sense of God's providence at work in the world at
large and in my world particularly. I cannot prove that, but I
know it. I have experienced it. And I have no doubt that God's
providence will also guide whatever the future bears. How can
I put this together? It's not easy.

The theologian in me says that the thrownness of existence keeps me from being forced to believe. I must move back
to God in and with my freedom. To see everything mesh in an
orderly, coherent, and purposeful way, which is the way of
providence, does not lead us to a free act of trust and surrender.
That clarity compels us to affirm God. Theologically, I can say
that there is a deeper wisdom behind the thrownness of existence that actually enables our freedom. That is the theological
reflection. Living the experience is another matter.

Existentially, I face a challenge not so easily settled by
theological reasoning. Loss is loss, chance is chance, and diminishment does not become enhancement. Existentially, the
challenge on my faith journey is to hold both honestly to the
thrownness of life and faithfully to the abiding providential
presence of God even in the thrownness. As I get older and the
stakes get higher, holding these elements together will, in the
end, be a work of grace and not my effort.

The Necessity of Religion and Church for Faith

I have dedicated my life to religion and to the Church as an
ordained priest. I live and work within religious structures,
organizations, institutions, and rituals shaped and sustained
by the Church. If something such as a sacrament is, as I believe,
not invented by the Church but instituted by Christ, still the

Church is responsible for its institutionalization, the specific embodiment of its contours. Great good has come from religion and the Church over time. Yet, both religion generally and the Church particularly must claim responsibility for actions and directions that have led to human diminishment—certainly not what God had in mind.

Again, as a function of growing older, I find more and more sources of disappointment in religion and the Church. As I see more good, I also see more limitations, failures, and even sinfulness. I can entertain the fantasy of what some have claimed as Martin Luther's vision of the Church—a purely spiritual fellowship of believers without the tawdry underside of institutional life. It is, however, a fantasy. It is unreal in the sense that it does not correspond to anything truly rooted in the earth and in human history. It is also a fantasy that disregards God's decision to take flesh in this world as it is, not an antiseptic and well-ordered world but a messy and wounded world.

Faith, I know, is not delimited by institutional structures. As I have reflected on my history, however, I cannot imagine faith sustained without those structures and without the human involvement that inevitably brings with it limitation and sin. It is no small challenge to hold fast to religion, Church, and faith all together. As I move forward, the lessons of history will gain even greater importance for me. Farewell words of Jesus will have their special power as well to sustain me: "Take courage; I have conquered the world!" (Jn 16:33b).

Growing Old and Growing Poor

It is blasphemy in my American culture at the beginning of the twenty-first century to embrace growing old and growing poor. Aging and impoverishment are antithetical to every contemporary aspiration for the good life right now. In faith, I welcome growing old and growing poor, because I know that these are necessary passages to an end moment that then, in a way I do not understand but accept, will open to an unimagined fullness of life and love. Growing old and growing poor is a kind of growing up finally.

In faith, I know this is true. I would never trade my current age for a younger one. I do not want to add more things to my life that will only clutter my final surrender into God's hands. In faith, I know this is true, but I must learn more about these realities of life and death and eternal life. I must understand more deeply. This is a challenge of faith, but it is also an exciting possibility. At times, I feel that it is a secret mission, hidden from younger cohorts and from people too busy acquiring things rather than seeking the truth.

For me, the excitement and adventure of this journey of faith stem from the journey's destination. Faith is bearing me into a future that I cannot begin to imagine. Faith has given me a glimpse of that future, but, for now, it remains out of sight. One day, however, I will move beyond faith to faith's destination: "Beloved, we are God's children now; what we will be has not yet been revealed. What we do know is this: when he is revealed, we will be like him, for we will see him as he is" (1 Jn 3:2).

What are the particular elements of faith that I set before myself as I grow older?

Part II

A THEOLOGICAL ACCOUNT OF FAITH

*Organizing and Understanding
Our Experience*

*M*y extended personal account of faith was an exploration of historical and cultural layers that have contributed to how I have come to be the believer that I am today. In giving this personal account of faith, I hoped to encourage your own personal exploration of the layers of your faith.

A personal and historical account of faith—what I have called an archaeology of faith—seems to be the right starting point. Here, a picture of faith emerges as a personal relationship with God. The experience of faith that comes into focus is a gift of God that corresponds to human yearnings and aspirations. It takes form as a personal relationship that finds expression in specific beliefs. Finally, the experience of faith can be clearly seen as a dynamic, living, and growing reality.

My personal account of faith belongs to me. Faith, however, is not idiosyncratic. At a fundamental level, faith is shared, even if its particular configuration is stamped for each of us by our particular history and circumstances. For that reason, a simple personal account of faith is insufficient to understand faith. We need something more than the archaeological retrieval of experience. We need ways to measure, discern, and organize the experience. For that purpose, a theological account of faith can serve us well. The theological account of faith will guide us in understanding how we share faith in common, even as we affirm the unique dimensions of our personal experience.

The doctrinal and theological presentation of faith—for example, in the *Catechism of the Catholic Church*—situates faith as a shared experience. A theological approach to faith can also organize personal experiences that may initially seem disconnected and even scattered. That theological gathering of faith experiences can render them more comprehensible. Finally, a doctrinal and theological account of faith helps to sift through various experiences and to discern what is of perennial value and what is not. Any account of faith, whether personal or theological, will always have the goal of fostering a deeper, wider, and truer experience of faith that not only takes root in the hearts of believers but enables them to grow and flourish in their relationship with God.

As we now begin a theological account of faith, we need to identify the resources that we will use for this account. The principal and guiding resource will be the Church's own understanding and synthesis of faith contained in the *Catechism of the Catholic Church*. Although the *Catechism* considers faith throughout its entire text, it does so in a more concentrated way in its first part, especially in numbers 26–197. In addition to the *Catechism*, we will draw from the theological writings of Juan Alfaro on faith.[1] Alfaro represents a reliable resource for the best of twentieth-century Catholic theological scholarship on faith.

As we move through our theological account of faith, we will begin with the foundations of faith. Then, we will consider the act of faith, the life of faith, and the consummation of faith in the vision of God. Finally, we will reflect on particular aspects that complete the theological portrait of faith.

Chapter 16

FOUNDATIONS OF FAITH: OUR CAPACITY TO RECEIVE GOD'S WORD AND BELIEVE

The deep foundation of our faith is our creation in the image and likeness of God (see Gen 1:27). To be created in God's image means that we are endowed with the ability to know and love, and so we can be in dialogue with the one who made us. God's image deep within us stirs our limitless desire and longing for absolute knowledge and complete love, a desire that only God can satisfy. In our very creation and constitution as human beings, we have a capacity or potential to be in relationship with God by faith. This capacity or potential establishes the human foundation for faith.

This ability to move beyond ourselves to God in faith is our openness to transcendence, which enables us to connect with and to enter into the very mystery of God. This capacity belongs not just to each of us alone. It is a shared human capacity that links us with every other human being in this world, each of whom is also created in the image and likeness of God. By our very nature, then, we can come to some natural knowledge of God. We can "read" the world and our human existence and come to know the transcendent presence of God.

St. Paul intimates this fact in his Letter to the Romans: "Ever since the creation of the world his eternal power and divine nature, invisible though they are, have been understood and seen through the things he has made" (Rom 1:20).

This knowledge, as wonderful as it is, still does not bring us into the intimate personal relationship of faith. Besides our natural capacity to reach for transcendence, and besides the marks of God's transcendent presence in the created world, something more needs to happen before we can enter into that intimate communion with God signaled by faith.

How has a kind of stretching and reaching beyond myself marked every layer of my experience of faith, even in its pre-Christian and pagan foundations?

Chapter 17

Foundations of Faith: God's Revelation and Self-Communication

*W*e cannot enter into communion with God unless God first reveals and communicates himself to us. We have the capacity or potential to receive the inviting and self-revelatory word of God, but unless that word is given, we cannot enter into the communion of faith.

In fact, God has taken that step toward us. God has revealed himself, and in that revelation he has communicated who he is for us. Even more, that revelation and self-communication become an invitation to share a life in communion with God.

The long trajectory of God's revelation and its culmination in Jesus Christ is the theme of the opening of the Letter to the Hebrews:

> Long ago God spoke to our ancestors in many and various ways by the prophets, but in these last days he has spoken to us by a Son, whom he appointed heir of all things, through whom he also created the worlds. He is the reflection of God's glory and the exact imprint of God's very being, and he sustains all things by his powerful word.

When he had made purification for sins, he sat down at the right hand of the Majesty on high, having become as much superior to angels as the name he has inherited is more excellent than theirs. (Heb 1:1–4)

Jesus Christ is the fullness of God's revelation. In speaking to us his Eternal Word, his Son, God could say and reveal no more. In his dialogue with Philip at the Last Supper, Jesus identifies himself as this full and complete revelation of God: "Whoever has seen me has seen the Father. . . . Do you not believe that I am in the Father and the Father is in me? The words that I say to you I do not speak on my own; but the Father who dwells in me does his works. Believe me that I am in the Father and the Father is in me" (Jn 14:9b–11).

How has God unexpectedly broken through the moments of my life and the lives of my ancestors in faith to invite us to deeper life and relationship?

Chapter 18

Our Response to God's Revelation: Our Act of Faith and Believing in God

*G*od reveals himself and communicates himself. The center of that revelation is Jesus Christ. Our response to God's revelation is to believe in God. We believe what God has revealed, because we believe in God who reveals it. In other words, we acknowledge and accept the truth of God's revelation. We do so on the basis of God, who is the guarantor of that truth. Faith accepts the truth of God's revelation in a free act of loving trust and surrender. We rely utterly and completely on God, who reveals himself. Besides being an affirmation of belief, then, our act of faith draws us into a relationship of trust and surrender with God, a communion with the one who has freely and graciously invited us to live in him through his revelation.

Our life of faith is coterminous with our life in this world. As long as we walk the earth, we live by faith. St. Paul says, "So we are always confident; even though we know that while we are at home in the body we are away from the Lord—for we walk by faith, not by sight" (2 Cor 5:6–7). Our destiny is not to stay forever on this journey of faith but rather to arrive where faith leads: the very vision of God. One day we shall not

137

believe God, but we shall see God. This is the sense of the First Letter of John: "Beloved, we are God's children now; what we will be has not yet been revealed. What we do know is this: when he is revealed, we will be like him, for we will see him as he is" (1 Jn 3:2). Faith's goal is not faith itself but the very vision of God and fully sharing in God's life, Father, Son, and Holy Spirit.

What has been the challenge of trust and surrender as I, perhaps sometimes painfully, became aware that I was walking "by faith, not by sight"?

Chapter 19

THE PROCESS OF FAITH: FROM THE ACT OF FAITH TO FAITH'S CONSUMMATION

*H*aving reflected on the basic and general contours of faith, we can profitably consider in greater detail how faith unfolds in our lives. In effect, this is a trajectory of faith in human experience—how it begins and how it arrives at its destination in the vision of God. The trajectory is a compressed phenomenology of faith as the Church has understood the threefold process of coming to faith, living and growing in faith, and arriving at faith's destination.

The Word Is Proclaimed

The famous phrase *fides ex auditu*, "faith from hearing," comes to us from St. Paul. It embodies the first step of coming to faith. The word is proclaimed or given. It is an external word identified with the Good News of Jesus Christ summoning all people to salvation. Here are Paul's words:

> But how are they to call on one in whom they have not believed? And how are they to believe in one of whom they have never heard? And how are they to hear without

someone to proclaim him? And how are they to proclaim
him unless they are sent? . . . So faith comes from what is
heard [*fides ex auditu*], and what is heard comes through
the word of Christ. (Rom 10:14–15a, 17)

The proclamation of the word in the Church began when
Jesus Christ commissioned his disciples. He entrusted to them
his mission, which they were to continue in the world. At the
end of Mark's gospel, Jesus gives the mandate to proclaim the
word that invites people to faith and through faith to salvation.
"And he said to them, 'Go into all the world and proclaim the
good news to the whole creation. The one who believes and is
baptized will be saved'" (Mk 16:15–16a).

---

*Who have been the bearers of the
word of Christ in my larger history
and in my personal life?*

God's Grace Interiorly Moves the Hearts of Those Who Will Believe

Faith is foremost a gift of God. It is also a graced and free human response to God's gift. The gift begins with the proclamation of an external word, the announcement of the Good News.
Then, as a person moves toward faith, another gift is necessary: the grace of God working within us. The gracious interior
movement of God opens our hearts, enables our freedom, and

makes us ready and willing to receive and accept the external word that has been proclaimed.

We find two very clear indications of this interior movement in sacred scripture. The first is in John's gospel. Jesus says, "No one can come to me unless drawn by the Father who sent me" (Jn 6:44a). The word "drawn" here clearly refers to the interior movement of God, which is indispensable in coming to believe in Jesus. The second reference is taken from St. Paul's ministry in Philippi described in the Acts of the Apostles. Paul goes outside the city gate to the river and preaches the word to a group of women. Among them is a woman named Lydia. The text describes Lydia listening to Paul's proclamation, which is an external movement. At the same time, an interior movement occurs: "The Lord opened her heart to listen eagerly to what was said by Paul" (Acts 16:14b). With the proclaimed word and the interior graced movement, she comes to faith and is baptized.

Can I name an experience I have had of interior illumination or even of some partial light?

Those Who Have Heard and Been Interiorly Moved Make an Act of Faith

Coming to faith or making an act of faith depends on the proclamation of the word and the interior movement of God's opening one's heart to receive that word. Then, in a free and fully human way, a person can make an act of faith and believe what God has revealed because that person accepts and trusts God's testimony and truthfulness. The believer now affirms the revealed truth and surrenders in trust and confidence to the revealer, who is God. In their act of faith, believers profess their faith, that is, *what* they believe, and simultaneously they acknowledge the source of their certain belief, that is, the one in *whom* they believe.

Affirming belief and affirming the one who stands behind the belief shape Paul's brief and powerful description of believing: "[I]f you confess with your lips that Jesus is Lord and believe in your heart that God raised him from the dead, you will be saved. For one believes with the heart and so is justified, and one confesses with the mouth and so is saved" (Rom 10:9–10). Both the Bible and the Church teach that the act of faith integrally affirms belief or the content of faith and, at the same time, enables us to enter into a relationship with God of communion in trusting surrender.

Can I name those moments of deep surrender in trust to God? Can I name the resistances to that surrender that threatened to hold me back?

The Life of Faith

The act of faith initiates a whole life of faith. This is the journey that deepens and expands our believing both in claiming more and more surely what we believe and in surrendering more and more completely in loving trust our very lives into the hands of God. This life of faith means our spiritual life, which grows and develops. Alternately, if it does not grow through grace-prompted cultivation, it will recede and wither. To speak of the life of faith also means that faith shapes both who we are and what we do. Faith has an eminently practical side.

The First Letter of John expresses the relationship of faith to our way of living in this way: "And this is his commandment, that we should believe in the name of his Son Jesus Christ and love one another, just as he has commanded us" (1 Jn 3:23). If we believe, then we act on and from our believing by loving one another. The Letter of James expresses the same relationship in different words: "What good is it, my brothers and sisters, if you say you have faith but do not have works? . . . [S]omeone will say, 'You have faith and I have works.' Show me your faith apart from your works, and I by my works will show you my faith" (Jas 2:14, 18).

Across time, the life of faith grows with God's help and our response to God's gift. Attention to the Word of God, devout participation in the sacramental life of the Church, the practice of personal prayer, seeking the counsel of wise and spiritual people, the exercise of merciful compassion to all we meet and especially toward the poor, the commitment to bring our faith to bear on our daily life, the cultivated readiness to surrender into God's hands especially in the face of loss and diminishment, our commitment to be an evangelizing person in the world who brings the Good News to those in need—all these disciplines and practices both indicate growth in faith and foster it.

How can I say that faith has grown in me? What does this look like?

The Consummation of Faith in the Vision of God

The life of faith is the journey of faith that reaches its destination in the vision of God. In the end, faith brings us home to God to share fully in God's own life. As Jesus invites his followers to believe in him, he also promises them this destiny: "Do not let your hearts be troubled. Believe in God, believe also in me. In my Father's house there are many dwelling-places. If it were not so, would I have told you that I go to prepare a place for you? And if I go and prepare a place for you, I will come again and will take you to myself, so that where I am, there you may be also" (Jn 14:1–3). Similarly, St. Paul contrasts our current condition on the journey of faith in this life with our future: "For now we see in a mirror, dimly, but then we will see face to face. Now I know only in part; then I will know fully, even as I have been fully known" (1 Cor 13:12).

The tension that results from being on a journey and not yet completing it explains a variety of experiences in the life of faith, from our hesitations to our struggles, from our joyful experiences of union to our dark nights of the soul. The life of faith is a work in progress. Its completion only happens in the vision of God.

What tests my journey of faith? What sustains it?

Chapter 20

PARTICULAR ASPECTS OF FAITH

$\mathcal{F}$aith comes to us both as God's gift and as our free human response. Knowing this, we begin to understand the richness and complexity of faith. As we consider particular aspects of faith, it becomes clear that these aspects inevitably reflect a "both-and" dimension. The following section will identify and describe some of these particular aspects of faith.

Faith: Doctrines but Also beyond Formulas

Many people—both believers and nonbelievers—see faith very reductively only as a set of doctrinal statements or propositions that are to be accepted as truth. In fact, doctrinal formulas are important articulations of faith, but they are not the direct object of faith. St. Thomas Aquinas made a very significant distinction. He wrote: "*Actus credentis non terminatur ad enuntiabile sed ad rem.*"[1]

The *Catechism* translates his words in this way: "The believer's act [of faith] does not terminate in the propositions, but in the realities [which they express]" (CCC, 170).

In other words, when we make an act of faith, our believing does not end in the affirmation of a proposition. We do affirm *something* as true, but we do so on the way to embracing the *one* who is true, that is, the *res* or the reality beyond and within the particular formula. More directly, faith leads us not to a statement but to divine mystery.

Doctrinal formulations have their place, and it is an important one. They give us an access to the mystery. They enable us to communicate with each other on matters of faith. They can be a reference point that indicates that we are moving in a right direction. For these reasons, the Church, her teachers, and her theologians care deeply about doctrine. They are concerned about its accuracy and its communicability. At the same time, doctrinal formulations are never absolute in themselves but are always instrumental and in service to connecting us with the mysteries that they name.

When or how did I realize that faith was not essentially information about God but a living and loving relationship with God?

Faith: Not Rational or Irrational but Reasonable

Is it mere wordplay to say that faith is not rational but that it is reasonable? Not at all. The distinction is critical to understanding the true nature of faith. Faith would be rational if it resulted from a process of empirical observation and reasoning. Evidence and logical connections would compel the affirmation of faith. In this scenario, freedom plays no role, just as freedom plays no role when I observe the sunrise and

judge that a new day has begun. The empirical evidence and
my reasoning compel me to arrive at the judgment that a new
day has begun. I have no choice in the matter. Faith, then, is
not rational in the sense of being the product of evidence and
reasoning that demand affirmation and exclude freedom. The
exclusion of freedom, as we will see, eviscerates the very heart
of real faith.

At the same time, faith is not irrational. Faith would be
irrational if it were opposed to reason and contradicted logic.
An irrational faith would lead us into a realm disconnected
with human ways of knowing and, for that matter, human
ways of loving. With irrational faith, we would attach ourselves for some inexplicable reason—perhaps a feeling of desperation or utter futility—to something that made no sense,
something foreign to human intelligence. Some call this form
of irrational and unreasonable faith "fideism," and its catch-
phrase is "Just believe." Irrational faith or fideism excludes an
essential element of our humanity, that is, our intelligence and
our capacity to know. With intelligence excluded, faith loses
its human dimension.

The Church understands that faith is neither rational nor
irrational, but rather that faith is reasonable. To say that faith
is reasonable means that what we believe and how we believe
is compatible with human ways of knowing. Faith does not
contradict reason, but, at the same time, it is not the product
of reason. The realities that faith affirms are not sensibly and
immediately evident, but neither do they contradict human
understanding. We cannot, for example, prove that we shall
rise from the dead by the power of Christ's resurrection. To
prove it would make it rational and deny its reality as a freely
embraced conviction. On the other hand, our intimations of

immortality, our longing for the fullness of life, and our abhorrence at the prospect of our personal extinction—all these suggest some coherence of the doctrine of the resurrection of the dead with human experience and understanding. Without that basic human coherence, faith in the resurrection of the dead would be a fideistic plunge into an irrational realm. If faith is to be free, it cannot be rational. If faith is to be human, it cannot be irrational. In the end, for faith to be real faith, it must be reasonable.

The reasonableness of faith indicates that faith is a human way of understanding. That affirmation, in turn, introduces us to the question of faith's certitude. Does faith give us knowledge that is certain and completely reliable? Can one have doubts and still believe? What about hesitations, difficulties, or questions?

Real doubt is the suspension of the judgment of the truth or falsity of something. In that sense, doubt is incompatible with faith, because the act of faith affirms truth. If we truly believe, we do not find ourselves in a state of suspension. We either believe or we do not; we either affirm what God reveals as true or we deny it. And if we affirm what God reveals as true, we do so on the basis of God testifying to the truth that we accept. If God is the guarantor, then what we believe must *certainly* be true. Faith, then, has no room for doubt and uncertainty. That would seem to close the matter. In fact, it does not.

We have heard St. Paul say that we walk by faith and not by sight and that we see things now through a mirror, dimly. We may believe without doubts but, while on this earthly journey, not necessarily with crystalline clarity. In fact, there is room for questions, hesitations, and even many difficulties, as

Cardinal Newman spoke of them: "Ten thousand difficulties do not make one doubt."[2]

The whole purpose of theology, as St. Anselm described it, is to seek understanding. Theology, he said, is *fides quaerens intellectum*, "faith seeking understanding." Were everything fully and transparently clear, there would be no need for a quest to understand faith.

The solidity of faith can perhaps be best understood in Pauline words from the Second Letter to Timothy, words that are frequently cited, as they appear in the Latin Vulgate edition: *Scio cui credidi et certus sum*, "I know the one in whom I have believed, and I am certain" (2 Tim 1:12; author's translation). The certitude and the reliability of faith originates in the one in whom we believe. At the same time, that "one in whom I have believed" is unfathomable mystery, who summons us to pass through our questions, hesitations, and difficulties to deeper and fuller understanding—until that day when in the presence of that great mystery we shall see God face-to-face.

How do I have "certain faith" because of my confidence in my relationship with God that does not need to be proved?

Faith: Free but Enabled

Beyond assent to particular truths, faith enters into a relationship of loving trust and communion with God. Entrance into that relationship, if it is to be true, must be free, because freedom belongs to the very nature of love, trust, and communion. Our relationship, again if it is genuine, can never be coerced or manipulated. In faith, we go to God and we do so freely. We are created and come from God, and we are returning to God. The only thing that we can give to God on that journey is our free assent in love. The Christian mystical tradition—for example, in the writings of St. John of the Cross, especially *The Ascent of Mount Carmel* and *The Dark Night*—insistently teaches the necessity of detachment from all that would impede us and render us unfree as we give ourselves over to God in faith.[3]

The sense of internal freedom that enables us to give ourselves over to God in trusting surrender is fundamental for the act of faith and the life of faith. An obvious correlative is freedom from external constraint. No one can force us to believe or to accept faith. Both interiorly and exteriorly, we embrace faith freely.

To affirm the necessity of internal freedom might seem to suggest that we go forward on our own power or by our own agency. In fact, our freedom is limited, conditioned, and imperfect. Our life experience clearly confirms that fact. Our internal freedom, as St. Paul insistently affirms in his Letter to the Galatians and again in his Letter to the Romans, is enabled and empowered by the great gift of our liberation in Jesus Christ. So Paul declares, "For freedom Christ has set us free" (Gal 5:1a). The empowering and enabling of our freedom in Jesus Christ means that our freedom in believing is truly *our* freedom but that it is also only possible because of God's gift or grace. From beginning to end, our faith, our act of believing, is ours and is also given to us as God's gift.

How can I honestly say that I have not felt forced to believe but rather free to believe, invited to believe?

Faith: Personal but Found and Lived in Community

The *Catechism* helpfully distinguishes between "I believe," the faith of the Church professed personally by each believer, and "We believe," the faith of the Church professed by the bishops assembled in Council or by the liturgical assembly of believers (CCC, 166). Faith, of course, is absolutely personal. No one can believe for us. To believe means that we have made a free and personal decision to accept what God has revealed and to surrender ourselves in confident love to God. At the same time, the *Catechism* reminds us that faith is not an isolated act:

> No one can believe alone, just as no one can live alone. You have not given yourself faith as you have not given yourself life. The believer has received faith from others and should hand it on to others. Our love for Jesus and for our neighbor impels us to speak to others about our faith. Each believer is thus a link in the great chain of believers. I cannot believe without being carried by the faith of others, and by my faith I help support others in the faith. (CCC, 166)

The community or social dimension of faith tells us that faith is an ecclesial or Church reality. As something that belongs to the Church, faith has its origins in the preaching of the apostles. The Lord Jesus commissioned them and entrusted them with the mission to proclaim the Good News to the whole of creation, to make disciples of all people, and to baptize them. The faith we profess is the apostolic faith. We are "members of the household of God, built upon the foundation of the apostles" (Eph 2:19b–20a). The faith proclaimed by the apostles is forever the reliable reference point for all generations that follow. Additionally, the apostolic ministry is continued in the Church, especially through the ministry of bishops in communion with the bishop of Rome, the pope. The Church, then, especially through the teaching office of the bishops, the Magisterium, is the authentic interpreter of the apostolic teaching and tradition. We return to our apostolic foundations, and as new circumstances arise we find Spirit-guided and reliable interpretations of faith through the Church's Magisterium.

The ecclesial dimension of faith is also evident in the Church's responsibility to evangelize, to proclaim the Good News to the whole world. Proclamation of the coming of the kingdom of God in the mystery of Jesus Christ is a summons to faith that constitutes the sacred purpose of evangelization. The word is proclaimed, so that the world may believe.

In his post-synodal apostolic exhortation *Evangelii Nuntiandi*, Pope Paul VI locates the task of evangelization, summoning people to faith, at the heart of the Church's identity. He writes:

> At the end of the great Assembly of 1974 we heard these illuminating words: "We wish to confirm once more that the task of evangelizing all people constitutes the essential mission of the Church." It is a task and mission which the vast and profound changes of present-day society

make all the more urgent. Evangelizing is in fact the grace and vocation proper to the Church, her deepest identity. She exists in order to evangelize, that is to say in order to preach and teach, to be a channel of the gift of grace (*Evangelii Nuntiandi*, 14). If evangelization is understood as "summoning to faith," then the Church or community dimensions of faith belong not only to a maintenance of fidelity but also to a dynamic outreach that wants to share faith with others, indeed, with the whole world.

How has a larger sense of history helped me to see faith emerging across time and in my own personal experience?

Faith: Given but Also Growing

Faith assents to the stable truth that God has revealed. Even more, faith enters into a stable and enduring relationship of trust and communion with God, who has revealed his truth and himself. Faith and its object, then, are given in a stable and reliable way. To remain faithful means, in the first place, to stay with the truth and to stay with the relationship that faith brings us. This commitment to the stability of faith moves Paul to his urgent and emotional exhortation to the Galatians:

> I am astonished that you are so quickly deserting the one who called you in the grace of Christ and are turning to

a different gospel—not that there is another gospel, but there are some who are confusing you and want to pervert the gospel of Christ. But even if we or an angel from heaven should proclaim to you a gospel contrary to what we proclaimed to you, let that one be accursed! As we have said before, so now I repeat, if anyone proclaims to you a gospel contrary to what you received, let that one be accursed! (Gal 1:6–9)

This strong language addresses a particular situation that belongs to the Galatians, but the underlying assumption is the stability of the truth of the gospel and the stability of the faith by which we embrace it.

These considerations of the stability of faith may give the impression that faith is merely a static reality. That is not so. Faith, in all its dimensions, contains a dynamism directed toward growth. Across the centuries, the entire Church experiences the development of doctrine, the dynamism of the truth of faith contained in the tradition. In a very important passage from the Second Vatican Council's "Dogmatic Constitution on Divine Revelation," we find this description of development:

The Tradition that comes from the apostles makes progress in the Church, with the help of the Holy Spirit. There is a growth in insight into the realities and words that are being passed on. This comes about in various ways. It comes through the contemplation and study of believers who ponder these things in their hearts. . . . It comes from the intimate sense of spiritual realities which they experience. And it comes from the preaching of those who have received, along with their right of succession in the episcopate, the sure charism of truth. Thus, as the centuries go by, the Church is always advancing toward the plenitude of divine truth, until eventually the words of God are fulfilled in her (*Dei Verbum*, 8).

The implications of the development of doctrine for individual believers are significant. If we can never say that we—as a Church or as a believing community—have fully and entirely grasped the truth that we hold in faith, then it makes sense that we might have significant questions, challenges, and even difficulties. Although the truth of faith is given and stable, while we are on this collective pilgrimage of faith and yet to arrive at our destination, we will no doubt recognize the incomplete unfolding of the faith to which we devotedly attach ourselves. In short, we are true believers who are also unsurprised that the divine truth must still grow clearer for us. We can wonder, and we can question, even as we remain loyal to our faith.

The dynamism of faith belongs not only to the collective experience of development in the Church; it also belongs to the heart of each individual believer. Throughout his letters, St. Paul insists that coming to faith is insufficient. One must also grow in that faith or, perhaps more accurately, let that faith grow in oneself. The following prayer taken from the Letter to the Ephesians expresses this personal dynamism of faith:

> For this reason I bow my knees before the Father, from whom every family in heaven and on earth takes its name. I pray that, according to the riches of his glory, he may grant that you may be strengthened in your inner being with power through his Spirit, and that Christ may dwell in your hearts through faith, as you are being rooted and grounded in love. I pray that you may have the power to comprehend, with all the saints, what is the breadth and length and height and depth, and to know the love

of Christ that surpasses knowledge, so that you may be filled with all the fullness of God. (Eph 3:14–19)

The personal dynamism and journey of faith that belongs to each believer is, in effect, his or her spirituality or spiritual journey. The spirituality of believers is that cultivation and growth in faith that makes us more and more fully who we are in God. It means an evermore expansive way of perceiving and understanding the world and ourselves in the light of faith. It means a fuller and deeper attachment to and communion with God and others in love. It means a greater readiness to make decisions and take action on the basis of faith. In short, spirituality is faith shaping the essential dimensions of our humanity in knowledge, connection, and action. The cultivation of spirituality and, therefore, of one's faith happens in attachment to the Word of God; participation in the sacraments; personal prayer; the practice of virtues, especially charity; and engagement with the community of faith, the Church.

As we understand the personal dynamism of faith, we also understand more clearly that coming to faith, the act of faith, is not only a point of arrival but also a point of departure for a lifelong journey of faith. We walk by faith and not by sight, but, indeed, we do walk on our way and toward our destination, which is the vision of God.

What have been some notable markers of growing faith in my larger history and in my personal experience?

Part III

Biblical Accounts of Faith

Expanding Our Experience

I began with a personal account of faith. It took the form of an archaeological excavation of faith that examined layer upon layer of history, culture, and personal experience in my family story of faith. Although this reflection focused on a large, long-term, and personal story of my faith, it was meant to evoke and illustrate experiences that we all share. Then, to organize that experience, to understand it, and to appreciate the common elements that connect it with the stories of others, we explored a theological account of faith. Now, in the final part of our reflections, we will consider several biblical accounts of personal faith. The purpose of retrieving biblical accounts of faith is to foster the expansion of our experience of faith.

At every juncture of our reflection on faith in history and in our personal experience, we came to know faith as a dynamic and growing reality. The experience of faith must expand, deepen, and grow as we journey in life and move toward faith's consummation in the vision of God. A static and lifeless faith is unsustainable and will eventually wither. So, there is some urgency in understanding the dynamic aspect of faith. The question is: How does that growth in faith happen?

An important clue for understanding growth in faith can be found in our personal and collective history of faith. How did we come to believe? Faith, as St. Paul says, comes from hearing (see Rom 10:17). Faith began with the Word of God proclaimed to us, the Word that we accepted. And that Word is present and available to us in a privileged way in sacred scripture. If the Word is at the origin of our faith, then the Word will also be the indispensable source of our growth in faith, if we return to it and listen attentively.

The Word of God contained in the scriptures has the ability to wake us up to new dimensions of faith, to illuminate faith in new life circumstances, and to move us to a deeper and wider act of loving surrender to God. The biblical Word of God, in short, is an essential and indispensable key to expanding our experience of faith.

The whole of the Bible represents a rich resource for our growth in faith. A particularly helpful approach can be found in identifying some specific personal narratives of faith within the Bible. These personal stories carry some continuity with these reflections, in which I have tried to retrieve and understand our unfolding personal experience of faith. Biblical narratives of faith, then, become invitations to reflect more deeply on our own faith. They also summon us to truer and deeper commitment. They are, in short, vehicles for expanding our experience of faith.

From among the many biblical accounts of faith, I want to propose for your consideration four faith stories drawn from John's gospel. The four stories belong to Nicodemus, to the Samaritan woman at the well, to Martha the sister of Lazarus at the time of his death, and to the apostle Thomas who encounters the risen Lord a week after his resurrection. It is not surprising that we find these four powerful stories of faith in John's gospel. Toward the end of his gospel, John explicitly identifies his purpose in writing—and it has everything to do with faith: "Now Jesus did many other signs in the presence of his disciples, which are not written in this book. But these are written so that you may come to believe that Jesus is the Messiah, the Son of God, and that through believing you may have life in his name" (Jn 20:30–31). We are continually "coming to believe," which is to say that we are continually summoned to grow and expand our faith.

Chapter 21

NICODEMUS: A BELIEVER IS REBORN

*N*icodemus appears three times in John's gospel. First, in chapter 3 (vv. 1–21), he approaches Jesus in the night and does so secretly. This nighttime encounter becomes a dialogue of the deepest kind about the very nature of salvation. Later, in chapter 7 (vv. 50–52), Nicodemus defends Jesus in the council of Pharisees. Finally, in chapter 19 (vv. 38–42), Nicodemus and Joseph of Arimathea bury Jesus after his crucifixion. We can consider these passages in detail and begin to identify Nicodemus's story of faith, a story that certainly belongs uniquely to him but also resonates with the stories of others, perhaps our own as well.

> Now there was a Pharisee named Nicodemus, a leader of the Jews. He came to Jesus by night and said to him, "Rabbi, we know that you are a teacher who has come from God; for no one can do these signs that you do apart from the presence of God. (Jn 3:1–2)

From the very beginning of the passage, we know that Nicodemus is a believer. Indeed, as a Pharisee, he is a devout and observant Jew. Nicodemus, like many contemporary believers, is deeply attached to his religious identity. At the same time, his visit in the night to Jesus suggests his awareness that there is something about faith that goes beyond the confines of his customary religious observances. Could it be—and this does happen to religiously minded people—that Nicodemus observes something new in the words and deeds of Jesus, and that novelty alerts him to the flatness of his own faith? Nicodemus may be like the conventional believer that many of us are, who begins to wake up to new dimensions of faith. Perhaps he is shaken from his conventional faith. He says to Jesus, "[N]o one can do these signs that you do apart from the presence of God." Nicodemus recognizes a fresh and powerful presence of God in Jesus. This recognition, this powerful and unusual intuition, mobilizes him to go to Jesus under the cover of darkness. His social position as a leader of the Jews and his public conventional faith do not permit him to engage Jesus openly in the light of day.

> Jesus answered him, "Very truly, I tell you, no one can see the kingdom of God without being born from above." Nicodemus said to him, "How can anyone be born after having grown old? Can one enter a second time into the mother's womb and be born?" Jesus answered, "Very truly, I tell you, no one can enter the kingdom of God without being born of water and Spirit. What is born of the flesh is flesh, and what is born of the Spirit is spirit. Do not be astonished that I said to you, 'You must be born from above.' The wind blows where it chooses, and you hear the sound of it, but you do not know where it comes from or where it goes. So it is with everyone who is born of the Spirit." Nicodemus said to him, "How can these things be?" (Jn 3:3–9)

Nicodemus's exciting intuition about expanded possibilities for faith turns into a stymied puzzlement when Jesus begins to speak of being "born from above." As often happens in John's gospel, those speaking with Jesus fail to grasp the meaning of his words. Nicodemus is caught in a literalism that leaves him unable to understand what Jesus is saying or to imagine what being "born from above" might look like. His question reveals his literalism and incomprehension: "How can anyone be born after having grown old? Can one enter a second time into the mother's womb and be born?"

Even today, faith struggles with literalism, which blocks the full truth and meaning of the message and a transformative encounter with Jesus. Some believers, for example, take hold of certain words of the Bible and claim to take them literally but actually read them through the lens of their own narrow categories. They do not grasp the true sense of the words, because they are held bound by their habitual experience and by their limited understanding. Their faith has a rote quality about it, and it always moves in predictable ways. Nicodemus takes the words of Jesus in this supposedly literal but actually distorted way. His question "Can one enter a second time into the mother's womb and be born?" reveals his brand of literalism.

Another kind of contemporary literalism about faith surprisingly comes from supposedly sophisticated quarters. Many contemporary nonbelievers, whether assertively atheistic or simply and quietly secularist in outlook, have a flat and literalist grasp of faith. They regard faith and religion as a mechanism to control others and to diminish their freedom, or perhaps as an easy source of solace or a projection of unmet needs, or as a remnant of childish magical thinking. You can easily hear them echoing Nicodemus's question: "Really? How can anyone be born after having grown old?" Life itself, for them, is literal. They might say, "Life is what is, and it amounts to no more than what you see, hear, feel, and touch right now. There is no chance to be born anew." Literalism in matters of faith crosses over conventional believers and nonbelievers alike. When we think that we know, we most probably do not.

Since Nicodemus is caught in literalism, we might expect Jesus to correct him with words such as these, "You have not grasped what I meant. Here is what I am really trying to tell you." Instead, Jesus insists on the utterly new, heavenly reality that is opening up before Nicodemus, a reality already antici-pated and glimpsed in Israel's history:

> Jesus answered him, "Are you a teacher of Israel, and yet you do not understand these things? Very truly, I tell you, we speak of what we know and testify to what we have seen; yet you do not receive our testimony. If I have told you about earthly things and you do not believe, how can you believe if I tell you about heavenly things? No one has ascended into heaven except the one who descended from heaven, the Son of Man. And just as Moses lifted up the serpent in the wilderness, so must the Son of Man be lifted up, that whoever believes in him may have eternal life." (Jn 3:10–15)

Regeneration, being born again in eternal life, belongs in a realm beyond "earthly things." That literal and earth-bound way of thinking can make no sense of "heavenly things." To know the presence of God, to enter the kingdom of God, to have eternal life beyond the inevitable death of earthly life—all this means breaking through the narrow boundaries of liter-al earthly thinking. Jesus invites Nicodemus into a new and

completely unimagined realm of eternal life. For Nicodemus—
and indeed for all of us—the only access to that new reality
that is named "regeneration," or being born again, is believing
in Jesus: "whoever believes in him may have eternal life." Our
relationship with Jesus is the only portal through which we can
pass into new understanding and, ultimately, regeneration.

The puzzled Nicodemus who only sees things in an
earthly way joins company with contemporary nonbelievers
who rely either on their own experience or the empirical and
measurable methods of science to come to truth about themselves and the world. Both Nicodemus and his contemporary
counterparts are limited by their literalism and one-dimensional thinking. Any breakthrough, if it is to happen, will occur
only when they crash through the boundaries of their thinking.
Jesus, who identifies himself as "the one who descended from
heaven," is that unique bridge linking earthly mortal existence
with heavenly regenerated life. That is his claim. He then verifies his claim with a proof not of logic and reasoning but of
love, as his words indicate:

> For God so loved the world that he gave his only Son, so
> that everyone who believes in him may not perish but
> may have eternal life. Indeed, God did not send the Son
> into the world to condemn the world, but in order that the
> world might be saved through him. Those who believe in
> him are not condemned; but those who do not believe are
> condemned already, because they have not believed in the
> name of the only Son of God. And this is the judgment,
> that the light has come into the world, and people loved
> darkness rather than light because their deeds were evil.
> For all who do evil hate the light and do not come to the

light, so that their deed may not be exposed. But those who do what is true come to the light, so that it may be clearly seen that their deeds have been done in God. (Jn 3:16–21)

Jesus verifies his identity as the access to regenerated or eternal life on the basis of God's love, which has given Jesus to the world. To know and experience that divine love reaching into our lives, crossing the boundary between infinite mystery and the human and mortal realms of this world—that is the verification of Jesus as our portal into a new way of knowing and a new birth.

A great question is posed in this teaching: Do I know—really know, beyond my capacity to understand—how the love of God has taken hold of my life and of the world?

The affirmation that God's love is linked to believing and eternal life adds a new note. In effect, Jesus tells Nicodemus that we had no choice in being born into this mortal life, this life that perishes. Once love enters the picture, however, so too does some choice, some exercise of freedom in reciprocating that love. Unlike earthy life that moves forward on its own terms and in its preconceived configurations, regenerated life born of love necessarily involves an act of freedom and decision. This decision is linked to believing in Jesus. It is a free response to God's love. It entails doing "what is true," and so "coming to the light."

When Nicodemus initially approached Jesus, he was intrigued by the works of Jesus that seemed to manifest the divine presence. Very quickly, Jesus draws him into a dialogue of deep dimensions. Jesus summons him to move beyond a narrow and conventional religiosity that keeps him locked in a literal mind-set. With a breathtaking pace, Jesus initiates him in the prospect of being born again, of being regenerated into eternal life. Jesus then leads him through the mystery of his own Incarnation as the one "who descended from heaven" and as the source of eternal life for those who believe. Divine love is the foundation of this new reality that Jesus sets before Nicodemus. And this divine love summons Nicodemus to a reciprocal love manifested in believing in Jesus and doing what is true by living in the light.

When Nicodemus departs from this nighttime encounter with Jesus, we are not certain whether or not he has fully grasped what Jesus has said. Perhaps he has grasped it but not accepted it. We do not know. We must wait for his second and then third appearance in John's gospel to know where he has gone on his journey of faith.

In chapter 7, John reports that the crowds were inclined to believe that Jesus was the Messiah. He then records the response of the religious authorities: "The Pharisees heard the crowd muttering such things about him, and the chief priests and Pharisees sent temple police to arrest him" (Jn7:32). Later in the chapter, the police return without an arrest. This sets the scene for an argument with the police and an eventual confrontation with Nicodemus, who appears at the end of the chapter.

> Then the temple police went back to the chief priests and Pharisees, who asked them, "Why did you not arrest him?" The police answered, "Never has anyone spoken like this!" Then the Pharisees replied, "Surely you have not been deceived too, have you? Has any one of the authorities or of the Pharisees believed in him? But this crowd, which does not know the law—they are accursed." Nicodemus, who had gone to Jesus before, and who was one of them, asked, "Our law does not judge people without first giving them a hearing to find out what they are doing, does it?" They replied, "Surely you are not also from Galilee, are you? Search and you will see that no prophet is to arise from Galilee." (Jn 7:45–52)

This brief passage does not give an account of Nicodemus's interior journey. The details about Nicodemus are few but telling. Nicodemus is identified as "one of them," that is, the Pharisees. Even so, he decides to take a countervailing position, so much so that it elicits a sarcastic remark, "Surely you are not also from Galilee, are you?" Nicodemus does not directly stand up for Jesus. Rather, he defends Jesus obliquely by invoking due process. More significantly, however, Nicodemus inches out publicly with his relationship to Jesus. In chapter three, he visited Jesus under the cover of night. Here, he offers a supportive albeit limited word in a public assembly. Although at this point we do not know the mind and heart of Nicodemus, his behavior strongly suggests that something has shifted or grown within him. Perhaps it is faith unfolding within him. Only in a final passage do we come to know the deeper reality of faith at work in Nicodemus.

The subtle signs of Nicodemus's growth in faith suggest that we take a closer look at ourselves. What are the signs of growth in faith in my own life? Do I have a greater willingness to entrust myself to God, or a greater openness to be more public with my faith?

The final appearance of Nicodemus in John's gospel occurs in chapter nineteen after the death of Jesus. The scene is the burial of Jesus.

> After these things, Joseph of Arimathea, who was a disciple of Jesus, though a secret one because of his fear of the Jews, asked Pilate to let him take away the body of Jesus. Pilate gave him permission; so he came and removed his body. Nicodemus, who had at first come to Jesus by night, also came, bringing a mixture of myrrh and aloes, weighing about a hundred pounds. They took the body of Jesus and wrapped it with the spices in linen cloths, according to the burial custom of the Jews. Now there was a garden in the place where he was crucified, and in the garden there was a new tomb in which no one had ever been laid. And so, because it was the Jewish day of Preparation, and the tomb was nearby, they laid Jesus there. (Jn 19:38–42)

In this dramatic scene of the burial of Jesus, we discover a detailed portrait of Nicodemus's faith. Nicodemus now gives public witness to his relationship with Jesus, as he and Joseph of Arimathea ask permission to take the dead body of Jesus away from the place of his execution. Nicodemus has moved from his visit by night to Jesus, to his tentative public defense of Jesus in the council of the Pharisees, to this dramatic public moment of caring for the dead body of the crucified Jesus.

Has Nicodemus truly come to believe in Jesus as Jesus presented himself to him in that first night visit as God's only Son who gives eternal life to those who believe in him? Or is this gesture of burying Jesus a simple sign of respect and honor rendered to a good man who was treated unjustly by the religious authorities? What are we to make of Nicodemus's action?

We can only understand Nicodemus and what he does if we fully grasp the reality of this moment. Jesus has died, and he has truly died. From all appearances, his death signals the collapse of all the great hopes and aspirations that people had placed in him. Collapse and definitive conclusion seem to mark this moment. Even if someone had believed in Jesus in the course of his lifetime, now that same person would be hard-pressed to persevere in faith, when death seems to rob faith of all its certainty.

The response of Nicodemus to the death of Jesus could have taken many forms. Nicodemus could have just walked away in disappointment. He could have rejoined the council of the Pharisees and concurred with them in their assessment of Jesus. He could have begun another religious search for another Messiah. He could have collapsed immobile in his own sadness. Instead of these possible responses, Nicodemus decided to bury Jesus. He did not need to bury Jesus. In fact, he risked his reputation by caring for the remains of someone who had been executed as a criminal and betrayer of religious tradition. In his action of burying Jesus, we find the key to understanding his faith.

The burial of Jesus can only be understood, especially in John's gospel, in light of Jesus' teaching found in chapter twelve. There, Jesus pronounces these words that described the mystery of his death and resurrection and the pattern that he shares with those who believe in him and follow him:

> The hour has come for the Son of Man to be glorified. Very truly, I tell you, unless a grain of wheat falls into the earth and dies, it remains just a single grain; but if it dies, it bears much fruit. Those who love their life lose it, and those who hate their life in this world will keep it for eternal life. Whoever serves me must follow me, and where I am, there will my servant be also. Whoever serves me, the Father will honor. (Jn 12:23–26)

The path to his glory, Jesus says, is in the earth where the seed dies and is buried and from which eternal life emerges. Those who want to share his glory and eternal life follow him, so that where he is, they also may be. To be born again into eternal life is to believe in Jesus. And to believe in Jesus is to join him in death and so to rise with him and by him into eternal life.

Nicodemus has come full circle. In that first visit by night to Jesus, Nicodemus learned that he needed to be reborn. He could not comprehend that possibility. It was linked, he learned, to the Son of Man who "must be lifted up"—lifted up, as he came to know, on the Cross, which is the path of death and leads to life eternal. To share that eternal life, Nicodemus needed to believe in Jesus and be reborn "of water and Spirit." As he now buries Jesus, he believes in the one who falls into the earth and dies to rise in glory. As he now buries Jesus, he believes in the one who draws him into glory and eternal life. At this moment, Nicodemus acts by faith and trust. He buries the dead Jesus, whose glory is not yet evident and whose risen life is not yet manifest. Even so, Nicodemus believes and knows beyond the literalism of death "that whoever believes in him may have eternal life" (Jn 3:16).

Nicodemus's narrative of faith begins with his conventional faith that is provoked by the works of Jesus to search for more. His encounter with Jesus leaves him more puzzled than enlightened. Gradually, faith in Jesus takes hold of him, until he participates—by faith—in the dying and rising of Jesus when he buries Jesus with Joseph of Arimathea.

When have I experienced those expansive moments of breakthrough, when I came to rest in a new sense of my relationship with Jesus?

Chapter 22

THE SAMARITAN WOMAN: THE UNLIKELY BELIEVER WHO BECAME A FERVENT EVANGELIST

*T*he fourth chapter of John's gospel narrates the lengthiest and most personal encounter that Jesus has with anyone. He meets and speaks with an unnamed Samaritan woman by a well at noontime. He is tired from a long journey and is sitting at Jacob's well in the city of Sychar. She comes in the heat of the day to draw water. He asks her for a drink, and that begins a dialogue that concludes in an altogether surprising and extraordinary way. Here is the account:

> A Samaritan woman came to draw water, and Jesus said to her, "Give me a drink." (His disciples had gone to the city to buy food.) The Samaritan woman said to him, "How is it that you, a Jew, ask a drink of me, a woman of Samaria?" (Jews do not share things in common with Samaritans.) Jesus answered her, "If you knew the gift of God, and who it is that is saying to you, 'Give me a drink,' you would have asked him, and he would have given you living water." The woman said to him, "Sir you have no bucket, and the well is deep. Where do you get that living water? Are you greater than our ancestor Jacob, who gave

174

us the well, and with his sons and his flocks drank from it?" Jesus said to her, "Everyone who drinks of this water will be thirsty again, but those who drink of the water that I will give them will never be thirsty. The water that I will give will become in them a spring of water gushing up to eternal life." The woman said to him, "Sir, give me this water, so that I may never be thirsty or have to keep coming here to draw water." Jesus said to her, "Go, call your husband, and come back." The woman answered him, "I have no husband." Jesus said to her, "You are right in saying, 'I have no husband'; for you have had five husbands, and the one you have now is not your husband. What you have said is true!" The woman said to him, "Sir, I see that you are a prophet. Our ancestors worshiped on this mountain, but you say that the place where people must worship is in Jerusalem." Jesus said to her, "Woman, believe me, the hour is coming when you will worship the Father neither on this mountain nor in Jerusalem. You worship what you do not know; we worship what we know, for salvation is from the Jews. But the hour is coming, and is now here, when the true worshipers will worship the Father in spirit and truth, for the Father seeks such as these to worship him. God is spirit, and those who worship him must worship in spirit and truth.' The woman said to him, "I know that Messiah is coming" (who is called Christ). "When he comes, he will proclaim all things to us." Jesus said to her, "I am he, the one who is speaking to you." Just then his disciples came. They were astonished that he was speaking with a woman, but no one said, "What do you want? or, "Why are you speaking with her?" Then the woman left her water jar and went back to the city. She said to the people, "Come and see a man who told me everything I have ever done! He cannot be the Messiah, can he?" . . . Many Samaritans from that city believed in him because of the woman's testimony, "He told me everything I have ever done." So when the Samaritans came to him, they asked him to stay with them; and he stayed there two days. And many more believed because of his word. They said to the woman, "It is no longer because of what you said that we believe, for we have heard for ourselves, and we know that this is truly the Savior of the world." (Jn 4:7–29, 39–42)

Nicodemus moved from conventional religiosity to a faith that immersed him in the dying and rising of Jesus and the mystery of his own regeneration. The Samaritan woman's journey to faith moves differently, and the difference is not surprising, because faith, for all the common elements that we share, is also stamped by our unique lives and experiences.

From the beginning, the Samaritan woman is an unlikely dialogue partner with Jesus. "How is it that you, a Jew, ask a drink of me, a woman of Samaria?" Her first steps toward faith begin in this improbable encounter between a Jewish man and a Samaritan woman. They are two people who seem so far apart. They are divided by cultural differences, by gender, and by different and entirely incompatible religious outlooks.

Who exactly is this Samaritan woman? The gospel offers few details of her life, but it suggests many clues. She is, for example, obviously a woman of a certain age. To have had five husbands and a current live-in boyfriend means that she has some maturity. At the same time, she cannot be very old. She labors under the daily grind of drawing and carrying water to her house. Most likely, she is also uneducated and unlettered, because that would have been the condition of nearly all the women in her social setting. Do not mistake, however, her lack of education for a lack of intelligence. She is quick-witted and knows, for example, how to shift the subject of a conversation with evident dexterity, especially when the conversation goes in the uncomfortable direction of her marital status. "Sir, I see that you are a prophet," she promptly replies to Jesus' revelation of her multiple marriages. She also demonstrates that she is religiously informed, when she contrasts the worship of the Jews and the worship of the Samaritans and when she articulates the hope of a Messiah to come. The text offers us these details and clues about the Samaritan woman, but there is more that marks her life at a much deeper level.

The Samaritan woman finds life burdensome. The drudgery of daily drawing water symbolizes her burdens. She is anxious for a solution or, at least, some relief, "Sir, give me this [living] water, so that I may never be thirsty or have to keep coming here to draw water." The routines of life and the hard-scrabble existence that belongs to people like her all contribute to her sense of weariness and even a depletion of life energy.

Besides a sense of burden, another important feature marks her life at a deep level. She is unsettled. The string of five husbands and then a current boyfriend tell us that she has lacked a fundamental stability in her life, and, with that, she has also lacked intimacy. Had she ever experienced a stable and sustaining love? It seems not. Then from this unsettledness and lack of intimacy, we can reasonably draw a line to sadness as an abiding feature of her life.

The Samaritan woman was no doubt a materially poor woman. She had no servant to go and fetch the water for her.

She had to do it herself. And there is another poverty she experiences, a lack of connection with others, something she might
not have been able to name but something that she certainly
experienced intensely. Perhaps that lack of connection enabled
her to accept the unlikely attention of a Jewish man at the well.
Perhaps her profound sense of disconnection made her open
and vulnerable when the moment came for this man Jesus to
invite her to speak with him and to give him water.

   If Nicodemus with his flat, literal, and conventional religiosity stands for people of the same stripe today, then the Samaritan woman also stands for and with an important segment
of contemporary experience. She is like many people today
who are disconnected at a deep level of spirit, even though
they may be sexually connected with many partners. For her
and for them, there is a search for intimacy that never quite
succeeds. This is symbolized in her solitary walk to the well to
draw water. She is also like many people today in her apparent
lack of self-knowledge and, certainly, lack of self-acceptance.
When Jesus unveils a part of her life, she seems taken aback
and quickly changes the subject. Today, many of our contemporaries have more information about themselves than they
are capable of processing, but few of them seem to grasp the
real truth of themselves in their dignity and in their need: in
the nobility of their creation in the image and likeness of God
and in their inner divisions and wounded souls.

---

*When has Jesus taken the initiative to meet
me in my solitude or aloneness, perhaps even
in my disconnection and isolation? How has*

*he taken the initiative? How has he drawn
me into a conversation, even in my reluctance?*

The encounter with Jesus draws the Samaritan woman to faith. We do well to pay close attention to the essential elements of that meeting, if we want to understand coming to faith, not just in a general way, but in how it might also take hold of our own lives.

The encounter between Jesus and the Samaritan woman is an intimate encounter, and he initiates it. For us, the word "intimacy," especially between a man and woman, immediately connotes some form of physical and sexual contact. In this encounter, the intimacy that Jesus initiates runs deeper than that. He quickly breaks through barriers when he asks for a drink of water. We know that thick cultural and religious barriers have been broached when we hear her astonished reaction, "How is it that you, a Jew, ask a drink of me, a woman of Samaria?"

Jesus is undeterred. He presses forward in the conversation. He says, "If you knew the gift of God, and who it is that is saying to you, 'Give me a drink,' you would have asked him, and he would have given you living water." The conversation advances, and Jesus asks her to call her husband. At that moment, he reveals his knowledge of her life, but, more than that, he reveals her vulnerability. Intimacy is about mutual disclosure, or revelation, and shared vulnerability. She stands before Jesus both revealed and vulnerable. In that, she is very much like another woman in John's gospel, the woman caught in adultery (Jn 8:1–11), whose sin is revealed and who is forced to stand before the religious leaders who are to decide whether she will live or die. Although the Samaritan woman's encounter with Jesus is not a public event as it was for the woman caught in adultery, she is still both revealed and vulnerable in her own situation. Jesus saves both women. Certainly he saves the woman caught in adultery; indeed, he saves her life and forgives her sin. But Jesus saves the Samaritan woman, too—yet, in a different way.

He knows her and reveals her in her vulnerability. He also reveals himself to her and makes himself close and vulnerable to her: "The woman said to him, 'I know that Messiah is coming. . . . When he comes, he will proclaim all things to us.' Jesus said to her, 'I am he, the one who is speaking to you.'"

What happens here? The woman experiences herself as known and accepted, and so she comes to faith in Jesus, knowing him to be the Messiah and so accepting him. "Come and see a man who told me everything I have ever done! He cannot be the Messiah, can he?" She has experienced an intimacy and a connection unlike any other in her life. In fact, the power of this intimate and connective faith is so great that she becomes a completely convinced and effective evangelist for her townspeople: "Many Samaritans from that city believed in him because of the woman's testimony."

When the woman of Samaria realizes that Jesus knows her completely in all her vulnerability and when she recognizes that God's Messiah accepts her, she believes—she comes to faith. For most people, the word "faith" has to do with knowing God. And that is true, as the last part of chapter four tells us when the townspeople speak to the woman: "It is no longer because of what you said that we believe, for we have heard for ourselves, and we know that this is truly the Savior of the world." To believe is to know God. To believe, however, also means that we are known by God. We have come to grasp that God's knowledge has flooded every corner and crevice of our lives. Nothing is hidden. We are known and, beyond that, we are received, accepted, drawn close.

This faith that brings together knowledge of God and knowledge of ourselves finds an echo in words of Paul. He speaks of the full trajectory of faith that unfolds across our lives and leads to the heavenly vision of God. He writes: "For now we see in a mirror, dimly, but then we will see face to face. Now I know only in part; then I will know fully, even as I have been fully known" (1 Cor 13:12). In that phrase "as I have been fully known," we catch the experience of the woman of Samaria who said, "He told me everything I have ever done."

What would it mean for me to grasp that God fully knows me and fully accepts me?

This Samaritan woman's story reverberates with so many pieces of contemporary experience. How many of us, like her trudging to the well every day, are just weary of the routines of our lives that seem to go nowhere? How many of us in the aftermath of the sexual revolution with its promise of quick and easy intimacy are as lonely as anyone ever has been? How many of us, like her, have strings of relationships that leave us unfulfilled and even empty? How many of us feel something akin to her isolation? How many of us feel disconnected and walled in by a virtual world of social media and electronic connections that never seem to bring us together?

If we meet a stranger who in a flash tells us all about ourselves and who knows us in every possible way—and who accepts us and draws us close—then we may come to faith as the Samaritan woman did. The possibility is not remote. Pray not to foreclose the conversation, as she did not. Let it unfold. Be ready to receive it. Then you will know as you are known.

The story of the Samaritan woman does not end with her coming to believe in Jesus. That is remarkable enough in itself, but there is more. She bears a word about him to her townspeople and effectively brings them to faith as well. "Many Samaritans from that city believe in him because of the woman's testimony." Faith, we begin to understand, cannot be self-contained. It radiates beyond personal experience and begins to touch others. Even more dramatically, it becomes a contagion. Yet, for faith to spread, it requires believers who will carry the message and possibility to the waiting world. That is what the woman does for her townsfolk. Jesus speaks of this collaboration in bringing people to faith in a conversation with his disciples, which is inserted in the larger passage about the woman (see Jn 4:31–38). He says, "But I tell you, look around you, and see how the fields are ripe for harvesting. The reaper is already receiving wages and is gathering fruit for eternal life, so that the sower and reaper may rejoice together" (Jn 4:35b–36). Faith takes hold of the Samaritan woman; and from her faith, the faith of others begins to grow.

Chapter 23

MARTHA: LOVE, DEATH, AND NEW FAITH IN JESUS

Chapter eleven of John's gospel tells the story of Jesus raising his friend Lazarus from the dead. This event provokes the chief priests and the Pharisees. They call a council to determine what to do about this Jesus, who is performing many signs that will, in their estimation, push the Romans to destroy their nation. They determine that it is best "to have one man die for the people" (Jn 11:50). The whole chapter is clearly about Jesus, and it serves as a prelude to the story of the passion and death of the Lord in subsequent chapters.

Still, there is another story that unfolds in this chapter, the story of Martha's faith. She is a sister of Lazarus and Mary and a beloved friend of Jesus. Martha's story of faith contains elements that belong to her. She comes to faith on her own path, one that is different from that of Nicodemus and the Samaritan woman. All three persons encounter Jesus and so come to faith, but each one meets him in a different way. Nicodemus comes to Jesus as a conventional believer and a religious authority. Jesus comes to the Samaritan woman whose faith is not fully formed. Jesus and Martha meet each other as friends by the tomb of her brother.

Many of us may identify with Martha, if Jesus is already a friend and a source of comfort and consolation. Like Martha, we may stand facing the pain and the limits imposed on us by death, and we may be seeking Jesus. In her grief and with questions and hopes of the deepest kind, Martha goes to meet this man she has known and known well. But she has not known him with a complete faith. She emerges from her encounter with Jesus as a person who has a newfound faith and a newfound relationship with Jesus, who is the resurrection and the life. It takes a crisis provoked by her brother's death and then a grace-filled meeting with Jesus to bring her to a depth of faith that she had never experienced. In this unfolding of her story, we may find ourselves invited to claim and complete our own faith—whether in the course of ordinary life or in moments of crisis. We can watch Martha and begin to see ourselves.

> Now a certain man was ill, Lazarus of Bethany, the village of Mary and her sister Martha. Mary was the one who anointed the Lord with perfume and wiped his feet with her hair; her brother Lazarus was ill. So the sisters sent a message to Jesus, "Lord, he whom you love is ill." But when Jesus heard it, he said, "This illness does not lead to death; rather it is for God's glory, so that the Son of God may be glorified through it." Accordingly, though Jesus loved Martha and her sister and Lazarus, after having heard that Lazarus was ill, he stayed two days longer in the place where he was. (Jn 11:1–6)

These verses set the scene for our reflection on Jesus' encounter with Martha. Clearly these words describe a set of close and loving relationships. The siblings are close to each other, and all three are attached to Jesus. Jesus, for his part, "loved Martha and her sister and Lazarus." Their closeness and reciprocal affection make it all the more puzzling that Jesus would stay away from them in a difficult time. Clues emerge in the following verses that give some insight into Jesus' decision to stay away.

> Then after this he said to the disciples, "Let us go to Judea again." The disciples said to him, "Rabbi, the Jews were just now trying to stone you, and are you going there again?" Jesus answered, "Are there not twelve hours of daylight? Those who walk during the day do not stumble, because they see the light of this world. But those who walk at night stumble, because the light is not in them." After saying this, he told them, "Our friend Lazarus has fallen asleep, but I am going there to awaken him." The disciples said to him, "Lord, if he has fallen asleep, he will be all right." Jesus, however, had been speaking about his death, but they thought that he was referring merely to sleep. Then Jesus told them plainly, "Lazarus is dead. For your sake I am glad I was not there, so that you may believe. But let us go to him." Thomas, who was called the Twin, said to his fellow disciples, "Let us also go, that we may die with him." (Jn 11:7–16)

Jesus' delay in going to visit the ailing Lazarus is reasonable, given the attempts of the religious authorities to kill him. Yet, he immediately indicates that line of reasoning is incorrect. His commitment is to walk in the light. There is no question of fear, even if the prospect of his coming passion and death is troubling. He is free, conscious, and deliberate as he moves forward. Later, in chapter twelve, he embraces his hour, which is his destiny in God's plan: "Now my soul is troubled. And what should I say—'Father, save me from this hour'? No, it is for this reason that I have come to this hour" (Jn 12:27). His raising of Lazarus will push Jesus' hour forward, as alarmed religious authorities recognize this great sign as an incitement of the crowds that will call down the Roman wrath and destruction upon them. There is a link between raising Lazarus and Jesus' own death, but this link is not the reason for his delay.

Jesus offers another reason consistent with a pattern from the very beginning of John's gospel, when he worked his first sign at Cana in Galilee: "Jesus did this, the first of his signs, in Cana of Galilee, and revealed his glory; and his disciples believed in him" (Jn 2:11). His intent now and his timing have to do with bringing people to faith. He says, "Lazarus is dead. For your sake I am glad I was not there, so that you may believe" (Jn 11:14b–15).

The scene is set now for the encounter of Jesus and Martha.

> When Jesus arrived, he found that Lazarus had already been in the tomb four days. Now Bethany was near Jerusalem, some two miles away, and many of the Jews had come to Martha and Mary to console them about their brother. When Martha heard that Jesus was coming, she went and met him, while Mary stayed at home. Martha said to Jesus, "Lord, if you had been here, my brother would not have died. But even now I know that God will give you whatever you ask of him." Jesus said to her, "Your brother will rise again." Martha said to him, "I know that he will rise again in the resurrection on the last day." Jesus said to her, "I am the resurrection and the

life. Those who believe in me, even though they die, will live, and everyone who lives and believes in me will never die. Do you believe this?" She said to him, "Yes, Lord, I believe that you are the Messiah, the Son of God, the one coming into the world." (Jn 11:17–27)

Martha's faith unfolds in stages. Notice, for example, her first step. She leaves the house filled with grieving mourners to go to her friend Jesus. She has called him, and she has placed her hope in him, even though the shape of that hope is not clear and precise: "But even now I know that God will give you whatever you ask of him."

In another step, Jesus elicits from her a profession of faith. Speaking of her brother, she says, "I know that he will rise again in the resurrection on the last day." This is the faith of the Pharisees (in contrast to the Sadducees), who affirmed a resurrection of the dead on the last day. Jesus then draws her to a new and extraordinary faith in him. He tells her who he is and then asks her a question: "I am the resurrection and the life. Those who believe in me, even though they die, will live, and everyone who lives and believes in me will never die. Do you believe this?" Jesus is no longer only a friend who has come in a moment of grief to console Martha. He now presents himself to her as the Lord of life and the one who has the power of resurrection. Then his question to her, "Do you believe this?" invites a response from Martha. The question, in its context, is extraordinary. He does not ask her, "Do you know this to be true?" Rather, he says, "Do you believe this? Do you trust me to be telling you the truth about life and resurrection?" Notice, too, that Jesus poses this question to her before he has performed a sign, worked a miracle, or given her some basis for belief. When Jesus asks Martha, "Do you believe this?" he summons her to affirm a truth and to trust in him—in other words, simply and purely to take him at his word.

Do you believe? When have I heard Jesus pose this question to me and so draw me into a wider and deeper faith?

Martha responds to Jesus with these powerful words: "Yes, Lord, I believe that you are the Messiah, the Son of God, the one coming into the world." Her response marks another significant step on her journey of faith. She moves from a loving and close friendship with Jesus into a new and extraordinary depth of relationship with him as her Lord and Savior, the incarnate One. As powerful and as profound as her affirmation is, Martha's faith, as subsequent verses tell us, is still a faith in formation.

> When she had said this, she went back and called her sister Mary, and told her privately, "The Teacher is here and is calling for you." And when she heard it, she got up quickly and went to him. Now Jesus had not yet come to the village, but was still at the place where Martha had met him. The Jews who were with her in the house, consoling her, saw Mary get up quickly and go out. They followed her because they thought that she was going to the tomb to weep there. When Mary came where Jesus was and saw him, she knelt at his feet and said to him,

"Lord, if you had been here, my brother would not have died." When Jesus saw her weeping, and the Jews who came with her also weeping, he was greatly disturbed in spirit and deeply moved. He said, "Where have you laid him?" They said to him, "Lord come and see." Jesus began to weep. So the Jews said, "See how he loved him!" But some of them said, "Could not he who opened the eyes of the blind man have kept this man from dying?" Then Jesus, again greatly disturbed, came to the tomb. It was a cave, and a stone was lying against it. (Jn 11:28–38)

Two strands are woven together throughout chapter eleven. The first is the humanity of Jesus captured in his love and friendship for Martha, Mary, and Lazarus. The other is his divinity, which establishes him as the life and the resurrection. Neither strand can be ignored, and both contribute to the story of Martha's faith.

Just after Martha's profession of faith in Jesus as "the Messiah, the Son of God, the one coming into the world," her sister Mary arrives. The verses that follow describe an intensely poignant human moment. Jesus, Mary, and Martha stand before the tomb of Lazarus together. Jesus feels the loss of Lazarus, and he weeps. The three of them share a moment of deep grief. The tomb is "a cave, and a stone was lying against it." The stone separates the three mourners from the mortal remains of Lazarus; it is emblematic of the barrier that death creates, the cold separation that it causes, and its seeming finality. They stand on the other side of the stone—and death seems to have had the last word.

This tableau of the three friends before the tomb tells us how closely Jesus connects with Martha and Mary in and through his humanity that shares the anguish of their loss. This human connection becomes the foundation of the deepest connection and relationship that they will have with Jesus in faith. In Patristic literature the humanity of Jesus is *organon salutis* or "the instrument of our salvation." In this moment of the passage, we recognize that Jesus' humanity is also the instrument of our faith.

Have you sensed that God knows your grief, the burden of sorrow that you carry? Has this been a prelude for your own deeper faith?

With his human relationship to Martha sealed in their connected grief, Jesus now begins to bring her to complete and divine faith.

> Jesus said, "Take away the stone." Martha, the sister of the dead man, said to him, "Lord, already there is a stench because he has been dead four days." Jesus said to her, "Did I not tell you that if you believed, you would see the glory of God?" So they took away the stone. And Jesus looked upward and said, "Father, I thank you for having heard me. I knew that you always hear me, but I have said this for the sake of the crowd standing here, so that they may believe that you sent me." When he had said this, he cried with a loud voice, "Lazarus, come out!" The dead man came out, his hands and feet bound with strips of

cloth, and his face wrapped in a cloth. Jesus said to them, "Unbind him, and let him go." (Jn 11:39–44)

When Jesus says, "Take away the stone," he begins to remove the barrier that death imposes on us. His words, however, invite an immediate reaction from Martha. For her, Lazarus's death is final. He is not only dead, but his mortal remains are already corrupting. "Lord, already there is a stench." Now Jesus is more than her loving friend who shares her grief; he speaks to her as her divine teacher: "Did I not tell you that if you believed, you would see the glory of God?" Her earlier profession of faith in Jesus as the resurrection and the life and as the Messiah and Son of God who is coming into the world comes to completion in response to Jesus' question, "Did I not tell you . . . ?" Martha is pressed to her human limits by that ultimate and universal limit of death. Martha is also graciously drawn by Jesus into the new reality of faith when he says to her, "[I]f you believed, you would see the glory of God." She responds now with a complete and trusting faith in Jesus, so complete and so trusting that it is beyond words. Martha's new faith is enacted in her obedience to the command of Jesus: "So they took away the stone." The raising of Lazarus follows.

Many of us are like Martha. We hear the summons to faith in the middle of our human condition, especially in its most fragile and vulnerable dimensions. The foundation for our nascent faith is our sense that God-in-Jesus is with us, knowing and sharing whatever marks our humanity. From that sense of human and divine connection, we hear a call to believe. It is a call to trust, to surrender, to acceptance, to reliance—in short, to everything that faith is, from accepting the truth that Jesus is the Messiah, the Son of God, to acting obediently to remove those barriers that block our full entrustment of ourselves into God's hands ("So they took away the stone").

For many of us, our faith begins in familiarity with Jesus, whom we know, at least in some measure. It moves forward as we recognize how he stands in solidarity with us in our humanity. It progresses even more each time we face those impossible limits that seem to stop us entirely. Then, we hear the question posed to us—perhaps many times across our life: "I am the resurrection and the life. Those who believe in me, even though they die, will live, and everyone who lives and believes in me will never die. Do you believe this?"

What are the impossible limits that summon me to deeper and fuller faith?

Chapter 24

THOMAS: THE APOSTLE OF CERTAIN FAITH

*E*ven those who are unfamiliar with the Bible know the phrase "doubting Thomas." In popular memory this apostle, also known as "the Twin," is permanently associated with doubt and a refusal to believe. All this is ironic. In John's gospel, Thomas eventually moves to absolutely certain and completely extraordinary faith. His narrative of faith does admittedly include hesitations, reluctance, and even refusal. He demands proof and will settle for nothing less than complete certitude. Although Thomas lives in the first century, his struggles with faith have a very contemporary ring.

A good place to begin reflecting on Thomas's story of faith is in the Farewell Discourse of Jesus. Thomas plays a minor but, in its own way, significant role in chapter fourteen of John's gospel. We read there:

> Jesus said, "Do not let your hearts be troubled. Believe in God, believe also in me. In my Father's house there are many dwelling places. If it were not so, would I have told you that I go to prepare a place for you? And if I go and prepare a place for you, I will come again and will take you to myself, so that where I am, there you may be also.

And you know the way to the place where I am going."
Thomas said to him, "Lord, we do not know where you
are going. How can we know the way?" Jesus said to him,
"I am the way, and the truth, and the life. No one comes to
the Father except through me. If you know me, you will
know my Father also. From now on you do know him
and have seen him." (Jn 14:1–7)

In the unsettled circumstances before his betrayal, arrest,
and crucifixion, Jesus summons his followers to faith. "Believe
in God, believe also in me." It seems at first that Jesus invites
two distinct acts of faith, one in God and one in him. That is not
the case. This faith, as the final words of the passage indicate,
is one. "If you know me, you will know my Father also. From
now on you do know him and have seen him." This singular
faith will become clearer later. For now, we need to pay attention to Thomas and his words.

As Jesus invites his disciples to faith and to confidence,
Thomas raises a difficulty and a question. "Lord, we do not
know where you are going. How can we know the way?" Unlike the other silent disciples who simply let Jesus' words pass
them by, Thomas feels compelled to challenge the summons to
faith. Unlike the others, he cannot "just believe."

When have I not been able "to just believe"?
How did the Lord draw me forward?

Jesus responds to Thomas not defensively but with a declaration: "I am the way, and the truth, and the life." Even more, Thomas's challenge prompts Jesus to explain more deeply how faith in him is divine faith: "If you know me, you will know my Father also. From now on you do know him and have seen him." He says, in effect, "In seeing me, you have seen the Father," as he will shortly explain to Philip. At this point, we do not know what impact Jesus' words have on Thomas. They have, however, set the stage for the Easter-evening encounter between Jesus and the disciples (minus Thomas), followed by another encounter with the disciples that includes Thomas, a week later. This account is in chapter 20. It reads:

> When it was evening on that day, the first day of
> the week, and the doors of the house where the dis-
> ciples had met were locked for fear of the Jews, Je-
> sus came and stood among them and said, "Peace
> be with you." After he said this, he showed them
> his hands and his side. Then the disciples rejoiced
> when they saw the Lord. Jesus said to them again,
> "Peace be with you. As the Father has sent me, so I
> send you." When he had said this, he breathed on
> them and said to them, "Receive the Holy Spirit. If
> you forgive the sins of any, they are forgiven them;
> if you retain the sins of any, they are retained."
>   But Thomas (who was called the Twin), one
> of the twelve, was not with them when Jesus came.
> So the other disciples told him, "We have seen the
> Lord." But he said to them, "Unless I see the mark
> of the nails in his hands, and put my finger in the

mark of the nails and my hand in his side, I will
not believe."

A week later his disciples were again in the
house, and Thomas was with them. Although the
doors were shut, Jesus came and stood among
them and said, "Peace be with you." Then he
said to Thomas, "Put your finger here and see
my hands. Reach out your hand and put it in my
side. Do not doubt but believe. [Do not persist in
your disbelief, but become a believer.[1]] Thomas
answered him, "My Lord and my God!" Jesus said
to him, "Have you believed because you have seen
me? Blessed are those who have not seen and yet
have come to believe." (Jn 20:19–29)

The first part of the passage describes the appearance
of Jesus to the disciples—minus Thomas—on Easter Sunday
evening. Jesus' appearance is mysterious. His risen body finds
walls and locked doors no obstacle. Could he be a ghost or a
phantasm conjured by the disciples' imagination? No, this is
truly bodily presence. He is the risen one who bears in his body
the marks of crucifixion, which he now shows his disciples.
He gives them a mission ("I send you") and an empowerment
for that mission ("Receive the Holy Spirit"). The response of
the disciples to this appearance of the risen Jesus is twofold.
They feel joy. "The disciples rejoiced when they saw the Lord."
Then, they are so obviously confirmed in their experience of
the risen Jesus, that they are ready to declare it directly and
unambiguously to the absent Thomas. "So the other disciples
told him, 'We have seen the Lord.'"

This passage describes the appearance of Jesus to the gathered disciples. He is visible to them, and they testify to that when they say, "We have seen the Lord." At the same time, the described event involves more than the disciples viewing an appearance of Jesus now risen from the dead, as remarkable as that might be in itself. Jesus is fully present to them in their gathering. He is present in many dimensions. They see him, and they also hear him. They feel his breath upon them as he invokes the Holy Spirit. They recognize a mission or responsibility that he entrusts to them. The disciples have a complete experience of Jesus fully present to them both exteriorly and interiorly. Finally, it is noteworthy that the disciples have this experience together, gathered in the house, or as the text says, "where the disciples had met."

Thomas was not part of the gathered community of disciples, even though the text specifies that he was "one of the twelve." Because he "was not with them when Jesus came," he did not share in their extraordinary experience. Thomas's coming to faith must begin when he rejoins the other disciples. This corresponds to the text, which says, "A week later his disciples were again in the house, and Thomas was with them." Here is a paradox in Thomas's narrative of faith and for many of us as well. Coming to faith is not only deeply personal; it is the most personal movement of our entire lives. And yet, we never make that personal journey entirely alone. In some form, a community of other disciples is both the context and matrix for our believing.

When were there moments when I felt "out of sync" with the believing community, even as I depended on their word of witness? How did I move forward?

When Thomas speaks with the other disciples after their experience of the presence of the risen Jesus, they tell him with what must have been great excitement, "We have seen the Lord." They offer him their testimony, or witness. Thomas does not outright deny their experience. Rather, he places a stringent condition of his own direct verification before he will accept what they say as true. He must identify the one whom they have seen and whom they claim as risen. He must verify that it is the crucified Jesus, or he will not believe them. "Unless I see the mark of the nails in his hands, and put my finger in the mark of the nails and my hand in his side, I will not believe."

The following week, when Thomas is with the other disciples in the house, "Jesus came and stood among them." Jesus takes up Thomas's challenge of verification and says to him, "Put your finger here and see my hands. Reach out your hand and put it in my side. And do not persist in your disbelief, but become a believer." In this powerful personal encounter with Jesus, in the midst of the assembled disciples, Thomas makes his profession of faith and declares, "My Lord and my God!"

Although Jesus invites him to put his finger in the nail marks and his hand in his side, Thomas does not do so. Thomas does not fulfill the conditions for faith that he had previously laid down. And, even more, the profession of faith that he does make is not about believing what the other disciples have told him. Clearly, when Jesus tells him to "become a believer," he is not telling Thomas that he should become a believer in what the disciples had told him. Jesus is calling Thomas to faith in him. And that, in fact, is the shape of Thomas's faith. When Thomas says, "My Lord and my God!" he believes in Jesus. The substance of that faith in Jesus far exceeds an acceptance of the disciples' witness that the crucified Jesus has arisen from the dead. With his eyes, Thomas sees the Jesus whom he has known and followed now alive. His profession of faith, however, goes even beyond a recognition that Jesus has risen from the dead. In faith, Thomas has seen in the risen Jesus his Savior and his God. That is both what he believes and the one in whom he believes: "My Lord and my God." The appearance of Jesus may occasion Thomas's profession of faith, and, at Jesus' invitation, he may even have had the means to achieve the verification that he once demanded. His faith, however, moves beyond the appearance of the risen Jesus and beyond the possibility of verification. His encounter with Jesus draws him into the mystery of his salvation by Jesus, whom he recognizes as Lord and as the author of his salvation, God.

In his profession of faith, Thomas has come full circle from his dialogue with Jesus at the Last Supper. Jesus had said to him, "I am the way, and the truth, and the life. No one comes to the Father except through me. If you know me, you will know my Father also. From now on you do know him and have seen him." In the risen Jesus and through his faith, Thomas now sees the face of God. Even more, he accepts what he sees and makes his profession of faith with the words: "My Lord and my God!"

How exactly does Thomas come to believe in Jesus as his Lord and God? The question is not merely academic or speculative. The reluctant and hesitant Thomas, who demanded a verification that he himself would execute, sounds very much like so many of our contemporaries, and maybe us as well. To understand his journey to faith could help people today. In fact, there is a mystery about Thomas's faith that makes it something not entirely explicable. There are, however, some elements that seem to be important contributors to his journey.

Thomas is gathered with other disciples. Jesus comes into that assembly and seeks out Thomas. The risen Jesus takes the initiative. Clearly, the other disciples who already believed in some way could not and did not engineer Thomas's faith. Now Jesus stands directly before Thomas and offers himself in an utterly intense and intimate encounter: "Put your finger here and see my hands. Reach out your hand and put it in my side." Jesus reveals his vulnerability—literally, his *vulnera*, or wounds. At the same time, Jesus risen from the dead has broken the great barrier imposed by death and reveals the power of God in the power of his own risen life. This conjunction of extreme vulnerability and infinite power of life puts Thomas before the mystery of the incarnate Word: "And the Word became flesh and lived among us, and we have seen his glory, the glory as of a father's only son, full of grace and truth" (Jn 1:14). This conjunction enables Thomas to know the truth of Jesus' words previously addressed to him: "If you know me, you will know my Father also. From now on you do know him and have seen him" (Jn 14:7).

If we are interested in fostering the faith of our reluctant, hesitant, and doubting contemporaries, we do well, first of all, to abandon all attempts to engineer their faith, that is, to dazzle them with incontrovertible arguments that will inevitably (in our minds) lead them to believe. Instead, if we present the mystery of Jesus Christ in all his vulnerability and all his glory, and if we let him take initiatives, our chances of success are much better, because we will be out of the way. If we try to make our contemporaries see the truth, if we try to force them to see the truth, we will paradoxically block it from their view. The blessedness of faith comes not with eyes that observe external realities and an intelligence that makes measured judgments. The blessedness of faith comes to those who have known the power and vulnerability of God beyond their sight, because it was revealed to them and they received it with open hearts. "Blessed are those who have not seen and yet have come to believe."

How does my faith grow in and through a direct encounter with Jesus? How does it grow with the support of a believing community?

Afterword

In a flash, at a trumpet crash,
I am all at once what Christ is, since he was what I am.

—Gerard Manley Hopkins, S.J.

*F*aith is amply rooted in history. The narrative that began in *Cuprae Fanum*, "Cupra's Temple," gives evidence of that. Faith urgently shapes this present moment—this now of questions and joys, hopes and dilemmas—with our holy and restless relationship with God. In the end, however, we know—at least as much as we can know—that faith from its very beginnings has been propelling us into an unexpected and unimagined future.

Faith, we also know, has introduced us to Jesus, into whose image we are being transformed. Sometimes we see his face brightly illuminated, and sometimes his presence—which remains and is real—becomes obscured by a painful darkness.

The way of faith, as we have come to know and experience it, is a pilgrim way. It unfolds across time and different terrains. It involves movement, usually forward but sometimes halting. It rejoices in small arrivals, and it grieves the struggle of crossing difficult spaces. It knows in hope the journey's destination—the transformation that has always been at work and that will come fully alive all at once, in a flash. Then we will be one with him who became one with us.

Notes

Chapter 8. The Church, the State and the Challenge of Faith

1. W. T. Selley, *Sixtus V: The Hermit of Villa Montalto* (Leominster, Herefordskire, UK: Gracewing, 2011), xi–xii.

2. Eamon Duffy, *Saints and Sinners: A History of the Popes* (New Haven: Yale University Press, 2006), 219; cited in Ibid.

3. Selley, *The Hermit of Villa Montalto*, xiii.

Chapter 10. *Teatro-dell'Arancio*, Orange Tree Theater

1. Pierre Teilhard de Chardin, *The Divine Mileu*, trans. Bernard Wall (New York: Harper & Row, 1960), 37.

2. Ibid., 39.

Chapter 13. Considered Faith

1. Juan Alfaro, S.J., *Fides, Spes, Caritas: Adnotationes in tractatum de virtutibus theologicis, new edition* (Rome: Pontifical Gregorian University, 1964).

2. John Henry Newman, *Fifteen Sermons Preached before the University of Oxford*, new edition, (London: Rivingtons, 1890), Sermon XII, n. 9, 259

Chapter 14. Transformed and Transforming Faith

1. Thomas Aquinas, *Summa Theologica* II-II, 1, 2, ad 2.

2. Teresa of Avila, *Collected Works, Vol. 1: The Book of Her Life*, trans. K. Kavanaugh and O. Rodriguez, 2nd edition (Washington, DC: ICS Publications, 1987), 194.

3. Ibid., 96.

4. Thérèse of Lisieux, *Story of a Soul: The Autobiography of Saint Therese of Lisieux*, trans. John Clarke, 2nd edition (Washington, DC: ICS Publications, 1976), 211–12.

5. Ibid., 213–14.

6. Ibid., 271.

7. Mother Teresa, *Come Be My Light: The Private Writings of the "Saint of Calcutta,"* ed. B. Kolodiejchuk (New York: Doubleday, 2007), 164.

8. Ibid., 210–11.

9. Ibid., 39–40.

10. Ibid., 99.

Chapter 20. Particular Aspects of Faith

1. Aquinas, *Summa Theologica* II-II, 1, 2, ad 2.

2. John Henry Cardinal Newman, *Apologia pro vita mea* (London: Longman, 1878), 239.

3. John of the Cross, *The Collected Works of St. John of the Cross*, trans. K. Kavanaugh and O. Rodriguez (Washington, DC: ICS Publications, 1979).

The last stanza of *Noche Oscura* ("The Dark Night") exemplifies this:

Quedéme y olvidéme
El rostro recliné sobre el Amado
Cesó todo, y dejéme,
Dejando me cuidado
Entre las azucenas olvidado

I abandoned and forgot myself,
Laying my face on my Beloved;
All things ceased; I went out from myself,
Leaving my care

Forgotten among the lilies.

Chapter 24. Thomas: The Apostle of Certain Faith

1. Translation by Raymond E. Brown, *The Gospel according to John (xiii-xxi)* (Garden City, NY: Doubleday, 1970), 1018–19.

Fr. Louis John Cameli is a Chicago Heights, Illinois, native and a priest of the Archdiocese of Chicago. He studied theology at the Gregorian University in Rome, where he received his licentiate in theology in 1970 and a doctorate in theology with a specialization in spirituality in 1975. Fr. Cameli is the author of more than a dozen books, including *The Devil You Don't Know: Recognizing and Resisting the Evil in Every Day* and *Catholic Teaching on Homosexuality: New Paths to Understanding*. He has been a contributor to *Chicago Studies, Priest*, and *America*. In 2001, he served as principal writer and general editor of the United States Conference of Catholic Bishops' document *The Basic Plan for the Ongoing Formation of Priests.*

Before and after his doctoral studies, Fr. Cameli served in two parish assignments. In 1975, he became professor of spirituality, director of spiritual life, and dean of theology at Mundelein Seminary of the University of Saint Mary of the Lake, Mundelein, Illinois. In 1996, Cardinal Bernardin appointed Fr. Cameli as director of ongoing formation of priests in the Archdiocese of Chicago and director of the Cardinal Stritch Retreat House in Mundelein. In 2002, he received the Blessed Pope John XXIII award from the National Organization for the Continuing Education of Roman Catholic Clergy for his contributions to the continuing education and ongoing formation of priests. In 2005, he was appointed pastor of Divine Savior Parish in Norridge, Illinois. In 2006, he received the National Catholic Educational Association's Seminary Department's John Paul II Seminary Leadership Award. In March 2009, Cardinal Francis George appointed Fr. Cameli as his delegate for Christian Formation and Mission with residence at Holy Name Cathedral, Chicago. Fr. Cameli has also served as a retreat director for priests' retreats and as a presenter for priests' convocations in the United States, Canada, and New Zealand.